Penguin Monarchs

THE HOUSES OF WESSEX AND DENMARK

Athelstan	Tom Holland
Aethelred the Unready	Richard Abels
Cnut	Ryan Lavelle
Edward the Confessor	James Campbell

THE HOUSES OF NORMANDY, BLOIS AND ANJOU

William I	Marc Morris
William II	John Gillingham
Henry I	Edmund King
Stephen	Carl Watkins
Henry II	Richard Barber
Richard I	Thomas Asbridge
John	Nicholas Vincent

THE HOUSE OF PLANTAGENET

Henry III	Stephen Church
Edward I	Andy King
Edward II	Christopher Given-Wilson
Edward III	Jonathan Sumption
Richard II	Laura Ashe

THE HOUSES OF LANCASTER AND YORK

Henry IV	Catherine Nall
Henry V	Anne Curry
Henry VI	James Ross
Edward IV	A. J. Pollard
Edward V	Thomas Penn
Richard III	Rosemary Horrox

THE HOUSE OF TUDOR

Henry VII	Sean Cunningham
Henry VIII	John Guy
Edward VI	Stephen Alford
Mary I	John Edwards
Elizabeth I	Helen Castor

THE HOUSE OF STUART

James I	Thomas Cogswell
Charles I	Mark Kishlansky
[Cromwell	David Horspool]
Charles II	Clare Jackson
James II	David Womersley
William III & Mary II	Jonathan Keates
Anne	Richard Hewlings

THE HOUSE OF HANOVER

George I	Tim Blanning
George II	Norman Davies
George III	Amanda Foreman
George IV	Stella Tillyard
William IV	Roger Knight
Victoria	Jane Ridley

THE HOUSES OF SAXE-COBURG & GOTHA AND WINDSOR

Edward VII	Richard Davenport-Hines
George V	David Cannadine
Edward VIII	Piers Brendon
George VI	Philip Ziegler
Elizabeth II	Douglas Hurd

DAVID WOMERSLEY

James II
The Last Catholic King

ALLEN LANE
an imprint of
PENGUIN BOOKS

ALLEN LANE

UK | USA | Canada | Ireland | Australia
India | New Zealand | South Africa

Allen Lane is part of the Penguin Random House group of companies
whose addresses can be found at global.penguinrandomhouse.com.

First published 2015
001

Copyright © David Womersley, 2015

The moral right of the author has been asserted

Set in 9.5/13.5 pt Sabon LT Std
Typeset by Jouve (UK), Milton Keynes
Printed in Great Britain by Clays Ltd, St Ives plc

ISBN: 978-0-141-97706-5

www.greenpenguin.co.uk

Penguin Random House is committed to a
sustainable future for our business, our readers
and our planet. This book is made from Forest
Stewardship Council® certified paper.

Contents

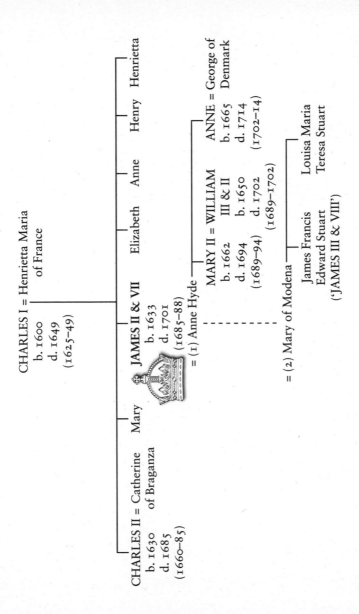

CHARLES I = Henrietta Maria
b. 1600   of France
d. 1649
(1625–49)

CHARLES II = Catherine   Mary   JAMES II & VII   Elizabeth   Anne   Henry   Henrietta
b. 1630   of Braganza   b. 1633
d. 1685   d. 1701
(1660–85)   (1685–88)
                                       = (1) Anne Hyde

                                       MARY II = WILLIAM   ANNE = George of
                                       b. 1662   III & II   b. 1665   Denmark
                                       d. 1694   b. 1650   d. 1714
                                       (1689–94) d. 1702   (1702–14)
                                                 (1689–1702)

                              = (2) Mary of Modena

                              James Francis   Louisa Maria
                              Edward Stuart   Teresa Stuart
                              ('JAMES III & VIII')

James II

I
The Varieties of Whig History

James II reigned for less than four years, from February 1685 to November 1688. Yet his short reign was one of the great pivots of English constitutional history. James ascended the throne with the formidable prerogative powers of the Stuart monarchy intact, and with Parliament as still a junior partner in the governance of the realm (Parliament had met for only eleven of the first forty years of the seventeenth century). After 1688 the prerogative powers of the crown, although still considerable, were acknowledged to be subject to parliamentary curbs. Furthermore Parliament itself had been transformed 'from an event into an institution', becoming a permanent part of the constitution, and one which met regularly.[1] The debacle of the end of James's reign, it has been said, was nothing less than 'a landmark moment in the emergence of the modern state', in which 'the character of English state and society relations was fundamentally transformed'.[2]

If James's brief reign was momentous in its political consequences at the time and during the following decades, it has for later generations proved to be no less of a battleground in English historiography. In 1931 the Cambridge historian Herbert Butterfield famously took aim at what he called 'the Whig Interpretation of History', a complacent teleological narrative in which the English nation had steadily advanced towards liberty, the rule of law and parliamentary democracy.[3] Butterfield's point was not to deny that these were in themselves very good things; simply that one could not regard them as the natural and necessary outcome of an historical process. The events of the reign of James II had played a cardinal role in the forging of this 'Whig Interpretation' during the eighteenth and nineteenth centuries. And, even today, the years 1685–8 present challenging campaigning territory over which historians of various stripes still engage with one another in displays of sometimes dazzling technical virtuosity.[4] However, it would be a mistake to think that there was only one kind of 'Whig Interpretation' of the reign of James II. To pause for a moment over the different kinds of Whig historiography will bring out the key issues which any account of the years 1685–8 must address.

Nine days after his defeat at the Battle of the Boyne the exiled James II landed at Brest and immediately began trying to persuade Louis XIV to entrust him with another army for the reconquest of his lost kingdoms. The campaign in Ireland, he urged, had depleted England of troops. Nothing could now withstand French forces, and furthermore his contrite people were eager to make amends for the disloyalty and ingratitude they had shown to their rightful monarch.

Louis was too polite to utter an outright refusal, but he was also resolved not to accede to James's request, and so he feigned illness in order that the unpleasant subject could not be raised. Macaulay describes the undignified position in which this left James:

> During some time, whenever James came to Versailles, he was respectfully informed that His Most Christian Majesty was not equal to the transaction of business. The highspirited and quickwitted nobles who daily crowded the antechambers could not help sneering while they bowed low to the royal visitor, whose poltroonery and stupidity had a second time made him an exile and a mendicant. They even whispered their sarcasms loud enough to call up the haughty blood of the Guelphs in the cheeks of Mary of Modena. But the insensibility of James was of no common kind. It had long been found proof against reason and against pity. It now sustained a still harder trial, and was found proof even against contempt.[5]

This portrait of James as a man both stupid and despicable is a dominant feature of Macaulay's *History of England*, which throughout lays a heavy emphasis on James's incurable faults of head and heart. James's Declaration of 1692 – a document consisting largely of lists of those of his former subjects, some designated by name, others designated more generally by reference to particular failures of conduct, who were to expect no mercy in the event of his restoration – Macaulay regarded as entirely characteristic: 'the whole man appears without disguise, full of his own imaginary rights, unable to understand how any body but himself can have any rights, dull, obstinate and cruel'.[6]

Macaulay's history of the reign of James and of the

Glorious Revolution which dethroned him was massively researched, as recent historians have acknowledged.[7] Nevertheless, its portrait of James as a man both mischievous and stupid, who attempted to remodel the institutions and character of England in a way that its people would never countenance, has paradoxical consequences. It makes the success of William of Orange in 1688 seem inevitable (which perhaps does less than justice to William's daring in launching such an audacious combined-forces operation in the depths of a northern European winter): 1688 was a notable staging post on the march of the English people towards the liberties Macaulay himself enjoyed in the mid nineteenth century. But it also makes the policies of James's reign seem inexplicable except as the product of almost unbelievable obtuseness on the part of the monarch. Finishing Macaulay's *History of England*, the reflective reader is liable to put down his book and ask the question, 'but why would anyone have tried, as James did, to reconvert England to Roman Catholicism, and to remodel its constitution on the lines of continental absolutist monarchies such as France?' By making the triumph of liberty and Protestantism a foregone conclusion, Macaulay is obliged to portray James as a Stuart King Canute (in the popular misunderstanding of that wise monarch's behaviour on the beach), who vainly attempted to turn back the resistless tides of history.

However, the accounts of Whig historians closer in time to the events of James's reign do not display Macaulay's complacency about the outcome of the historical process.

The 'Preface' to the *Quadriennium Jacobi, or the History of the Reign of King James II* of 1689 is characteristic. The subtitle – 'From his first Coming to the Crown to his Desertion' – is sufficient evidence of the Whiggish standpoint from which the history was written, since it was a cardinal objective of the Whigs following James's flight to France to have this deemed an abdication (or desertion).[8] The author of the *Quadriennium* is as persuaded as Macaulay would be 150 years later that James was mischievous and misguided: '*Seldom do we find a President of any Prince that laboured, against all the Common Rules of Policy, so industriously to lose a Crown, when he had once fix'd it on his Head, as* James II.'[9] But what James rashly and wickedly attempted was not, to this contemporary, as ridiculously impractical as it would appear to be to Macaulay. For those who experienced them, the religious and political policies of James's reign were marked by a terrifying, violent energy: '*nor did he gradually and insensibly endeavour to introduce his Innovations of Popery and Slavery, but rush'd and broke in like a Torrent with open and armed violence upon the Ancient Constitution of the Nation.*' As a result, James very nearly succeeded in subverting '*the* British *Monarchy, the Glory whereof was almost brought to utter Ruin and Destruction*'.[10]

Which of these kinds of Whig history – the massively untroubled Victorian Whiggism of Macaulay, or the more hysterical seventeenth-century Whiggism of the *Quadriennium* – is closer to the truth? Did James, out of a mixture of stupidity and malice, attempt the impossible, as Macaulay implied?

Or were the religious and political objectives of his reign not only feasible (albeit in the end unwelcome to a majority of his subjects), but in fact very nearly achieved? Were they even, perhaps, not as wicked and 'un-English' as both Macaulay and the author of the *Quadriennium* would brand them?

2
Duke of York

CHILDHOOD, CIVIL WAR AND EXILE

The future James II was born on 14 October 1633 at St James's Palace, the second son of King Charles I and Henrietta Maria of France. He was baptized by the Archbishop of Canterbury, William Laud. He was named after his grandfather, James I and VI, whose pet project of the uniting of the crowns of England and Scotland was also recalled in the titles bestowed on him: the dukedoms of Albany and York. He spent his early years in Richmond Palace, where his governor was William Seymour, Marquess of Hertford. His tutors included, at various times, the suave High Church bishop and Oxford don Brian Duppa, William Harvey, Dr Broughton and a 'Mr Croucher'. However, the young prince was no natural scholar, preferring physical activity to study. In 1647 his father would be forced to urge him to 'ply his book more and his gun less'.[1]

With the outbreak of the Civil War in 1642 the refined life James had enjoyed from birth was interrupted. The previous year the children of the royal family had witnessed angry crowds in Whitehall demanding the head of Charles I's principal minister, the Earl of Strafford. Once relations between the king and Parliament had broken down, and it was clear that their disagreements about the governance of the kingdom would be referred to arms, James's life was suddenly full of incident. In April 1642 he was temporarily held as a hostage by the Parliamentarian governor of Hull, Sir John Hotham. In October of the same year he and his elder brother were present at the Battle of Edgehill, where late in the day they had a narrow escape from a party of Parliamentary horse which might have 'destroyed or taken prisoner the King himself, and his two sons, the prince and the duke of York, being with fewer than one hundred horse and those without officer or command'.[2]

Following Edgehill the Royalists withdrew to Oxford, which then became their capital: 'a centre of operations in the Thames valley, a centre of government, the domicile of that part of the court that was not away with the King and, finally, the spiritual home of Royalism, the stronghold of Archbishop Laud's brand of High Anglicanism'.[3] While his father and elder brother were frequently absent promoting the Royalist cause, James remained in Oxford. But over the next three years the tide of war set in favour of the Parliamentarians, and on 25 June 1646 Oxford surrendered. Charles I had cast himself on the mercy of the Scots, and James's elder brother, Prince Charles, had fled to France. James became a captive of the Parliamentarians and was sent to London. There he was reunited with his younger brother and sisters and committed to the custody of the Earl of Northumberland in St James's Palace. This was no harsh restraint. James would later tell Gilbert Burnet, the clergyman and subsequent adviser to William of Orange, and whose *History of His Own Time* is rich in vivid detail, that Northumberland 'had used him with great respect'.[4]

In the spring and summer of 1647 Charles I was first passed from the Scots to the Parliamentarians, and then kidnapped by the army and held initially at Maidenhead, subsequently at Hampton Court. During that summer those of the royal children still in the country were allowed to visit their father. In these meetings Charles urged his children to be loyal to their elder brother, to have no truck with any Parliamentarian attempts to vary the succession in their favour, and – ironically, given James's eventual actions – always to adhere to the Church of England.[5]

The failure of Charles's attempt to escape to France in 1648 resulted in closer confinement for James, who nevertheless began to make more serious attempts himself to escape to the safety of the Low Countries, as his father had suggested he should, and where his sister Mary was married to William II of Orange.[6] In these schemes he was encouraged and assisted by the Presbyterian army officer and Royalist spy Joseph Bampfield. By mid April their plans were ripe. James absconded from St James's Palace at night, met his associates in the park, disguised himself in women's clothing and headed down river by barge. The refugees met up with a Dutch vessel in the mouth of the Thames, which transported them to Flushing, where they landed on 23 April 1648.[7] In the circumstances of this adventure one can glimpse oddly scrambled anticipations of the events of forty years later, when James would again flee from England by

boat and in disguise, driven from his throne by the son of
the very sister and brother-in-law who were now welcom-
ing him so warmly to the Hague.

The life of the exiled Stuarts conformed to the general
pattern of such courts. Sources of money were irregular,
precarious and never sufficient for the expense necessary to
keep up the show and dignity of royalty. The various house-
holds which comprised the court – that of the queen and
those of Charles and James – engaged in ceaseless manoeuvring and backbiting. Faction was ubiquitous. On one
side were the moderate Royalists, whose principal leader
was Edward Hyde (later Earl of Clarendon, Lord Chancellor under Charles II, historian of the Civil War and the
father of James's first wife, Anne). Against the moderates
were ranged a group of 'ultras' attached to the queen, who
were more focused on ends and less troubled by means.
Both Charles and James had at times a difficult relationship
with their mother, whose interference in their affairs they
resented. A particular flashpoint arose when she attempted
to convert their younger brother Henry to Roman Catholicism: an attempt that James would later claim to have
foiled.[8] Interestingly, at this point in his life, although he
was rumoured to display at least a sensuous affinity with
Roman Catholicism, James disavowed both any interest in
that religion, and any understanding of how one could pos-
sibly be interested in it. It is reported that his father had
commanded him to obey his mother in all things 'except in
matters of religion'.[9]

As for James's relationship with his elder brother, although
they were at times close and affectionate, their dealings with

each other were also strained as a result of the machinations and bickering of their servants, as well as of the afterlife of occasionally sharp conflicts.[10] Burnet would conclude that Charles had always hated James, although the record does not really support so simple a view.[11] Nevertheless, a bitter quarrel in 1656 in the Spanish Netherlands, when Charles had obliged James to quit the French army, and James had defied Charles by retaining the services of Sir John Berkeley, still rankled with both men as late as 1667.[12] Charles was reputed always to have been more fond of his younger brother, Henry Duke of Gloucester.[13]

The execution of Charles I in January 1649 was a devastating blow, and one that decisively shaped James's understanding (or perhaps one should say misunderstanding) of the times through which he lived. In the first place, the execution of his father confirmed James in a very simple belief about the motivations of those who withstood the wishes of the house of Stuart. The regicides were nothing more than disaffected republicans, and consequently principles derived from either religion or more nuanced ideas of monarchy had played no part in guiding their actions. Still less had they been surprised by the turn of events and driven to more or less desperate improvisations. James was absolutely certain that it was 'a republic which is at the bottom of all these affairs in England and not religion'.[14] As Burnet was later to comment: 'He was bred with high notions of the Kingly authority, and laid it down for a maxim, that all who opposed the King were rebels in their hearts.'[15]

Secondly, James distilled from his father's fate a very simple lesson about kingly conduct. Although he had been close to his father, he nevertheless believed that Charles had in some way brought disaster upon himself. If only he could have been more resolute in resisting the moves made by the Parliamentarians against his loyal servants Strafford and Laud, all might have ended well. James inferred that inflexibility was the only kingly response to opposition; and, furthermore, those who were opposed to monarchy never aimed at anything less than a thorough extirpation. Charles Fox put his finger on the perversity of this inter-pretation of the fate of Charles I: 'both the sons of Charles, though having their father's fate before their eyes, yet feared not to violate the liberties of the people even more than he had attempted to do'.[16] What Talleyrand would later brilliantly say of another ejected royal house, the Bourbons – 'ils n'ont rien appris, ni rien oublié' – might be applied with equal accuracy to James II. Like the descendants of the French monarch who would eventually give him sanctuary, he too was condemned to be able neither to forget, nor to understand, his own experience. That blindness to the subtlety, at times even the contradictoriness, of human motivation which could, in the end, bring fundamentally loyal and well-affected subjects to 'so desperate a passe'[17] as to acquiesce in, even perhaps to desire, revolution; and that calamitous simplification of kingly conduct to the single rule of unbendingness – these were principles that would serve James ill in the great crisis of his reign in 1688. The problems with James's conduct when king lay not in the abstract legality of what he attempted, nor even in the pol-itical theory of the ideas of monarchy and of the obligations of the subject on which he based his actions. Rather, they lay in his naive assumption that facts in the realms of legal and political theory could be translated without loss into the realm of political practice.

For James seems never to have understood the conditionality of all political authority and of all political obedience, even where both power and obedience are characterized in the most absolute terms. A little less than a century later, in the midst of a crisis in which an English administration was once again inclining to trust too much to abstract questions of right, it would be Burke who would try to educate his contemporaries in these great political truths. Conditionality is a law which rules with equal imperiousness both those who govern –

> Despotism itself is obliged to truck and huckster. The Sultan gets such obedience as he can. He governs with a loose rein, that he may govern at all; and the whole force and vigour of his authority in his centre, is derived from a prudent relaxation in all his borders.[18]

– and their subjects:

> When you drive him hard, the boar will surely turn upon the hunters. If that sovereignty and their freedom cannot be reconciled, which will they take? They will cast your sovereignty in your face. No body will be argued into slavery.[19]

James would never stoop to truck and huckster. Even the apparent flexibility of the latter part of his reign – the famous 'reversal of alliances' which saw him seeking the support of the previously despised Whigs and Dissenters – was dictated and required by his intransigence over objectives. Nor did he ever manage to grasp that there were limits to passive obedience.

The principal opportunity with which exile on the continent furnished James was the chance to see military action in the French army alongside the greatest general of the day, Turenne. It was an experience which stirred in him a 'strong inclination to acquire more and more experience in the art of war'.[20] He took part in the 'hot attack' on Étampes, was present at the siege of Mouzon, and served in the front line at the siege of Arras. Following the treaty between France and the English Protectorate in 1655, James reluctantly quit the French army, although he quickly found another outlet for his martial energies. Early in 1657 he enlisted in the Spanish army, which obliged him to fight against his former patron and mentor, Turenne, and involved him in the defences of Mardyck, Dunkirk and Nieuport. At the Battle of the Dunes on 14 June 1658 he led his troop of cavalry with great gallantry, but was obliged twice to retreat. In all these actions James acquitted himself well, drawing from no less a judge of military conduct than Condé the praise that 'if ever there was a Man in the World without Fear, it was the Duke of *York*'.[21]

Yet James's memoirs of this period contain details that re-echo with a curious dissonance in his later life.[22] He pays lavish tribute to Turenne's virtuosity as a general, in terms which show that he was aware of how presence of mind, a willingness to abandon preformed plans and an ability to improvise under pressure were vital to the successful exercise of military command. But James was unable to duplicate these virtues in his own conduct in 1688, and seems never to have grasped that an unswerving adherence to a plan, no matter what the circumstances, can show foolishness rather than resolution. (Indeed, when he became king James would choose, unerringly, both the wrong moments to be flexible and the wrong moments to be unbending.) He recognized that Turenne's success was due in part to his mastery of the more technical aspects of the art of war, such as forced marches. Again, in 1688 James would be unable to put that lesson into practice. Finally, the memoirs record an aristocratic *contretemps*, when at a council of war James had quarrelled with Don John de Toledo over a point of strategy. When asked by the Prince de Condé why he had done so, James answered that 'he had no mind to be forced a second time to run away as at the battle of the Downs'.[23] The ironies require no underlining. Burnet would later puzzle over how James's later conduct could agree so ill with his youth: 'in the end of his life he came to lose the reputation of a brave man and a good Captain so entirely, that either he was never that which flatterers gave out concerning him, or his age and affairs wrought a very unusual change in him'.[24]

When all seemed beyond hope for the exiled court, the implosion of English politics following the death of Cromwell brought about what had been (in the words of John Evelyn) 'past all humane policy'. On 16 May 1660 a formal invitation to return was issued to Charles II. On 29 May the new king entered London in triumph, to the unfeigned joy it would seem of the great majority of his subjects, as Evelyn recorded:

> This day came in his Majestie Charles the 2d to London after a sad, and long Exile, and Calamitous Suffering both of the King and Church: being 17 yeares: This was also his Birthday, and with a Triumph of above 20000 horse and foote, brandishing their swords and shouting with unexpressable joy: The wayes straw'd with flowers, the bells ringing, the streetes hung with Tapissry, fountaines running with wine: . . . I stood in the strand, and beheld it, and blessed God . . . for such a Restauration was never seene in the mention of any history, antient or modern, since the returne of the Babylonian Captivity, nor so joyfull a day, and so bright, ever seene in this nation . . .[25]

RESTORATION

The Restoration of the monarchy transformed James's position. He was of course still very much under the sway of his elder brother. But that position of dependency, which was to endure for another twenty-five years, was nevertheless softened by access to much greater supplies of money. At the Restoration Parliament had granted James a present of £10,000.[26] By 1663 his income was some £47,000 per annum (although his expenditure greatly exceeded his income, rising to £75,000). Yet over the next few years his income would also rise strongly. He received revenue from the post office and from wine licences;[27] as Lord Admiral he participated in the profits from prizes (a strong source of wealth during the Dutch wars);[28] and he also received rents from his Irish estates. Moreover, James seems to have managed his household well. In 1667 the French ambassador reported that his 'servants are paid punctually, and he owes nothing'.[29] Burnet would concur: 'He was a frugal Prince, and brought his Court into method and magnificence.'[30]

However, James also now had a greater need of money, since his personal circumstances had changed. During the later 1650s he had begun an affair with Anne Hyde, the daughter of the future Lord Chancellor and historian of the Civil War. She was then in the service of James's sister Mary. On the eve of the Restoration, Anne had discovered that she was pregnant. After lengthy pestering from James, Charles eventually gave his permission for the two to marry, though this was hardly the glittering and, above all, useful dynastic match that might have been expected for the brother of the king. Anne had genuine personal qualities: Burnet would praise her as 'a very extraordinary woman. She had great knowledge, and a lively sense of things.'[31] But in birth she ranked far below James.

The ceremony of marriage was performed privately on 3 September 1660 by James's chaplain, Dr Crowther. James was still racked by doubts and second thoughts: there was no public announcement. A son was born on 22 October and was acknowledged by James. On 2 November the queen arrived from France, determined to break up the marriage.[32] For a while James wobbled, browbeaten by his mother and unsettled by rumours of Anne's earlier promiscuity. But Charles was adamant that the marriage could not be undone, and so on 20 December James publicly acknowledged Anne as his wife. Over the following eleven years she gave birth to seven children, most of whom – including all the sons – did not survive. Burnet's suspicions concerning the birth of James's son and heir many years later were roused by his discouraging track record as a sire:

> The children were born with ulcers, or they broke out upon them soon after: And all his sons died young, and unhealthy. This has, as far as any thing that could not be brought in the way of proof, prevailed to create a suspicion, that so healthy a child as the pretended Prince of *Wales* could neither be his, nor be born of any wife with whom he had lived long.[33]

As well as his new wife James kept several mistresses (in 1666 Pepys would note that James was 'becoming a slave to this whore Denham'), and that commitment to pleasure, together with his regular fox-hunting, often distracted him from 'care of business', as Pepys also complained.[34] James's judgement in women did not raise his standing in the eyes of his contemporaries: 'He was perpetually in one amour or other, without being very nice in his choice: Upon which the King said once, he believed his brother had his mistresses given him by his Priests for penance.'[35]

As well as additional income, the Restoration had brought James important public responsibilities. He had been Lord Admiral since the age of three, but it was only now that he could properly discharge the duties of that high office. In his *Diary* Pepys repeatedly praised James's understanding of, and application to, naval business, noting with approval that 'the Duke of Yorke doth give himself up to business and is like to prove a noble prince; and so endeed I do from my heart think he will'.[36] Burnet agreed that James 'came to understand all the concerns of the sea very particularly', but went on to note a doctrinaire quality to James's policies as Lord Admiral which foreshadowed the more unfortunate choices he would make when king:

> The Duke found, all the great seamen had a deep tincture from their education: They both hated Popery, and loved liberty: They were men of severe tempers, and kept good discipline. But in order to the putting the fleet into more confident hands, the Duke began a method of sending pages of honour, and other young persons of quality, to be bred to the sea. And these were put in command, as soon as they were capable of it, if not sooner. This discouraged many of the old seamen, when they saw in what a channel advancement was like to go; who upon that left the service, and went and commanded merchantmen. By this means the vertue and discipline of the navy is much lost.[37]

James's duties as Lord Admiral were not merely administrative. In 1665 he commanded in person at the Battle of Lowestoft, where a Dutch fleet was defeated, and where he had been in the very thick of the action:

> The Earl of Falmouth, Muskery, and Mr. Rd. Boyle killed on board the Dukes ship, the *Royall Charles*, with one shot. Their blood and brains flying in the Duke's face – and the head of Mr. Boyle striking down the Duke, as some say.[38]

It was an incident which drew a slightly more tart response from that disaffected Parliamentarian and poet, Andrew Marvell, who grasped the opportunity for a witty glance at James's reputation for slowness of mind:

> His shatter'd head the fearless Duke distains,
> And gave the last first proof that he had Brains.[39]

Notwithstanding such slurs, James was vigorous and active in the early and mid 1660s. He sat on the Council of Foreign Plantations as well as the Navy Board, and he involved himself with energy in colonial trade, being the patron of both the Royal African Company and the East India Company.[40] During the Great Fire of 1666 both he and the king took a lead in the dangerous work of containing the blaze: 'labouring in person, and being present, to command, order, reward, and encourage Workmen; by which he shewed his affection to his people, and gained theirs.'[41] Burnet – surely not an historian likely to magnify James's talents or virtues – nevertheless praised the many good qualities in the character of the young Duke of York: 'till his marriage lessened him he really clouded the King, and pass'd for the superior genius. He was naturally candid and sincere, and a firm friend, till affairs and his religion wore out all his first principles and inclinations. He had a great desire to understand affairs: And in order to that he kept a constant journal of all that pass'd, of which he shewed me a great deal.'[42]

This way of life was shaken by the disaster of 1667. On 12 June a Dutch raiding fleet broke the chain at Chatham, sailed up the Medway, captured and towed off as a prize the *Royall Charles*, one of the principal ships of the navy, and burned several others. The consequences were shame at the woeful state of neglect and unpreparedness that the Dutch incursion had exposed, and panic at what might happen next: 'never were people so dejected as they are in the City all over at this day, and do talk most loudly, even treason; as, that we are bought and sold, that we are betrayed by the papists and others about the King ... They look upon us as lost; and remove their families and rich goods in the City and do think verily that the French, being come down with his army to Dunkirke, it is to invade us – and that we shall be invaded.'[43]

Someone would have to take the blame for this humiliation, and the choice of a sacrifice to 'attone the people' fell on James's father-in-law, Lord Chancellor Clarendon, whose windows had been broken by the mob on 14 June.[44] It was in some ways desperately unfair. Clarendon had opposed the current war with the Dutch, and he bore no responsibility for the dismal state of military neglect that the Dutch raiders had revealed. 'Unjust and ungrateful' were the words Burnet would use to characterize Charles's behaviour in abandoning his principal minister.[45] But Clarendon was no longer so indispensable as once he had seemed to be, and so on 30 August he was dismissed.

The disgrace and subsequent impeachment, flight and banishment of Clarendon clearly created difficulties for James, who had initially been willing to abandon him, but who in the end was 'very strong for his father-in-law at this trial'.[46] Nevertheless, the fall of Clarendon 'lessened' James, as Pepys recognized.[47] Moreover, it also brought about an estrangement between the two brothers, as Pepys learned from a chance encounter with Thomas Povey, a fellow civil servant and the Treasurer for Tangier:

> Thence I into St. James's park and there met Mr. Povy; and he and I to walk an hour or more in the Pell Mell, talking of the times. He tells me, among other things, that this business of the Chancellor doth breed a kind of inward distance between the King and the Duke of York, and that it cannot be avoided – for though the latter did at first move it through his folly, yet he is made to see that he is wounded by it, and is become much a less man then he was, and so will be. But he tells me that they are, and have always been, great dissemblers one towards another . . .[48]

Charles's new favourite was the witty, malevolent Duke of Buckingham, an inveterate enemy of Clarendon's and therefore also a foe to James: 'Clarendon's enemies – notably Henry Bennet, Earl of Arlington, and George Villiers, second duke of Buckingham – were determined to ensure that he did not return from exile and resume power. They were therefore eager to drive from office and from the court all who might support Clarendon's return, among whom James and Anne were the most conspicuous. To this end they sought to make Charles jealous of his brother's influence and ambitions and to supplant him from his position as heir presumptive. One possibility was that Charles might vest the succession in his son James Scott, duke of Monmouth, but there was no doubt that Monmouth was illegitimate, so a more promising expedient seemed to be for Charles to divorce the queen on the grounds of sterility.'[49] The coming years would bring a changed political landscape, fraught with new perils.

CONVERSION

The fall of Clarendon, the consequent decline of his former adherents and the rise of Buckingham and Arlington, who were busily encouraging Charles towards innovative and unscrupulous new methods of trying to control Parliament, would by themselves have made the years following 1667 problematic for James. However, the greatest source of adversity James encountered in the years leading up to his accession in 1685 arose as a result of an act entirely of his own choosing, namely his conversion to Roman Catholicism.

The bare facts of James's conversion are easy to state. Early in 1669 he had contacted the Jesuit Fr Simons to explore the practicalities of a conversion to Roman Catholicism. In particular James was concerned to know whether or not the pope would allow him to conceal his conversion and continue publicly to attend the services of the Church of England. Simons said that this would not be possible, and there matters rested for a while, with James being unable to take the final step. It was not until the spring of 1672 that he was received into the Catholic Church (although he continued to attend Church of England services for another four years).[50] Even then James's Catholicism, though a matter of common knowledge and easily inferred from his conduct, was not official until 1676, when the pope acknowledged his conversion.[51] And even as late as 1679, during the cut and thrust of the national crisis created by parliamentary attempts to exclude James from the succession, there were apparently some who were prepared to contend that it 'was not yet legally certain, that the Duke was a Papist'.[52]

The background to and motivation for James's conversion are, however, matters of much more absorbing interest and – from the standpoint of the interpretation of his actions once he became king – of much greater historical importance than the simple chronology. In 1647 Charles I had commanded his children to obey their mother – a Catholic – in all things except the choice of religion, requiring them always to adhere to the Church of England. Both James's Roman Catholic hagiographers and his radical Whig detractors agreed, however, that he had wasted little time in betraying his father and adopting the religion of his mother. After James's death the Jesuit Brettonneau would praise the benign influence of the queen on her children:

He [James] was Born in the Protestant Religion, and had been Instructed in it; but Divine Providence made him find that in the Queen his Mother, which would Correct the Unhappiness of his Birth, and former Education. The Care which this Virtuous Princess took to Inspire the Princes her Children with favourable Thoughts of the Catholick Religion, and to show 'em the Errours which they had suck'd in with their Milk, cast the first Seeds into the Duke of *York*'s Mind, which the Divine Grace afterwards made use of to Work out his Conversion with: And the Correspondence he held with the Catholicks in *Flanders*, contributed still more to the strengthning those good Impressions which he had receiv'd in France . . . it was not long before he was perfectly

Disabus'd. He read the History of the *Pretended Reformation* of the Church of *England*, Compos'd by Dr. *Heylin*, and found the Remedy in the very Source of the Distemper. It pleas'd God to enlighten him, and show him the false Principles of the Error wherein he was unhappily Ingag'd ... though he was already a Catholick in his Heart, yet he had no Mind to do any thing Rashly; and therefore conceal'd his Sentiments at first, and communicated them only to the King.[53]

A number of points are worth underlining here. In the first place, Brettonneau insists that James was receptive to the influence of the queen. (James himself, however, would deny this in the letter on the subject of his religion he wrote to his daughter Mary.)[54] Secondly, although the timings in this account are vague, Brettonneau seems to locate the moment of inward conversion to the 1650s and during James's residence in Flanders. Thirdly, he acknowledges a period of concealment and dissimulation.

The account of James's conversion composed shortly after his flight from England in 1688 by the radical Whig author of the scandalous *Secret History of the Reigns of Charles II and James II* agrees in many respects with that written by the Jesuit, although of course what the latter admires the former deplores, adding for good measure a treasonable political motive for James's conversion:

'Tis well known, and a thing confirm'd by two Letters yet to be seen, wherein one of the King's own Chaplains, then upon the spot when it was done, imparts and laments it to a

> Bishop, That *the Duke of* York, *while he was yet but very young, made a solemn Renunciation of the Protestant Religion, and was reconciled to the Church of* Rome *while he sojourned with his Mother in* France, *in hopes by the assistance of the Papists to have defeated his elder Brother of his Right of Inheritance, tho he had all the Indulgence imaginable to conceal his Conversion, where it might be for his private Advantage, and the general good of the Cause.*[55]

However, there are good grounds for believing that both the radical Whigs and the Jesuits – for very different motives, of course – simplified and flattened the process of James's conversion. Inward stirrings towards Roman Catholicism may have begun early, but it is going too far to suggest that in the 1650s James's confessional disposition was either entirely settled, or harnessed to nefarious political ambition. Conspicuous piety was a demeanour he acquired only after 1688, and his loyalty to Charles seems only rarely, if ever, to have wavered.[56]

The most circumstantially detailed account we have of the origins and growth of James's inclination towards Roman Catholicism is provided by Gilbert Burnet, whose portrait is more psychologically nuanced, and employs milder, more varied, more human and more believable colouring:

> He gave me this account of his changing his religion: When he escaped out of the hands of the Earl of *Northumberland*, who had the charge of his education trusted to him by the Parliament, and had used him with great respect, all due care was taken, as soon as he had got beyond sea, to form him to

a strict adherence to the Church of *England*: Among other things much was said of the authority of the Church, and of the tradition from the Apostles in support of Episcopacy: So that, when he came to observe that there was more reason to submit to the Catholick Church than to one particular Church, and that other traditions might be taken on her word, as well as Episcopacy was received among us, he thought the step was not great, but that it was very reasonable to go over to the Church of *Rome*: And Doctor *Steward* having taught him to believe a real but inconceivable presence of *Christ* in the Sacrament, he thought this went more than half way to transubstantiation. He said, that a Nun's advice to him to pray every day, that, if he was not in the right way, God would set him right, did make a great impression on him. But he never told me when or where he was reconciled.[57]

That his conversion was a work of time, to which James's own reflections contributed as much as the advice of others, and also that it was in part nourished by the very doctrines and traditions of the High Church Anglicanism in which James had been bred – these are plausible touches which redeem James's conversion from the simplified caricatures of both the Whigs and the Jesuits.

Further corroboration of Burnet's milder and more believable interpretation comes from the religious character of James's home life at this period. His wife had been 'bred to great strictness in religion', and had followed a form of High Anglicanism positioned, in terms of doctrine and ritual, on the very boundary with Catholicism. From the age of twelve she had practised secret confession with George

Morley, later Bishop of Winchester, whose churchmanship was perhaps opposed more to nonconformity than to Catholicism: Burnet reports him as being 'zealous against Popery, and yet a great enemy to the Dissenters'.[58] As early as 15 April 1668 Pepys had seen how things were moving in the religious lives of the duke and duchess: 'Thence to White hall by water and there with *D[uke of] Y[ork]* a little but stayed not but see him and his lady at his little pretty chapel where I never was before but silly devotions God knows.'[59] In the late 1660s, just as James's inclinations towards Catholicism were strengthening, so the duchess seemed also to be moving in the same direction:

> It was observed, that for fifteen months before that time [March 1671] she had not received the sacrament; and that upon all occasions she was excusing the errours that the Church of *Rome* was charged with, and was giving them the best colours they were capable of. An unmarried Clergy was also a common topick with her.[60]

Although she denied it to Morley, who apparently cross-examined her on the subject, Anne had decided to become a Roman Catholic by the spring of 1670, and James had encouraged her in that resolve, sharing with her his reading of Peter Heylin's sceptical history of the Reformation: 'He had taken Care that the same Book which upon the Reading of it had made so much Impression upon himself, should, as it were by Chance, light into the Dutchesses Hands; she read it, and was Touched with her own Reflections which she made as she Read it.'[61]

However, her death on 31 March 1671, as described by Burnet, suggests that her faith may finally have trembled. At her bedside was Walter Blandford, then Bishop of Oxford, formerly her father's chaplain. He expressed the hope that she 'continued still in the truth: Upon which she asked, what is truth: And then, her agony encreasing, she repeated the word Truth Truth often: And in a few minutes after she died'.[62] To quote Pontius Pilate is no unambiguous sign of enduring faith.[63] But any wavering at the end does not alter the fact that, in the months preceding her death, she and her husband seem each to have reinforced the religious journey of the other.

It was a journey on which Charles himself had also embarked. In December 1668 the king had begun a course of instruction, and on 25 January 1669 (the feast of the conversion of St Paul) he had discussed being received into the Catholic Church with Lord Arundell, Sir Thomas Clifford and Arlington. In Charles's case, however, this desire to embrace Roman Catholicism, whatever its origins, quickly degenerated into a bargaining chip in his ongoing negotiations with France, from whom he needed money: an arrangement sealed by the secret clauses of the Treaty of Dover in 1670.[64] Even the French were eventually undeceived on the point of Charles's religion, the Archbishop of Rheims remarking to Burnet in 1684 that 'the King was as much theirs as his brother was, only he had not so much conscience'.[65]

But although Charles's religious motivation was probably shallower and more instrumental than that of his brother, it nevertheless contributed to a rising tide of suspicion among the population at large concerning Roman Catholicism in the royal family. It was a tide which the Declaration of Indulgence of 1672, suspending the execution of all penal laws against both Catholics and Nonconformists, did nothing to lower: 'When the Declaration for Toleration was published, great endeavours were used by the Court to persuade the Nonconformists to make addresses and complements upon it. But few were so blind, as not to see what was aimed at by it.'[66] James was a particular focus of this suspicion: 'he lost the Affection of the *English* so soon as they begun to perceive that he had chang'd his Religion, or had a Mind to do't'.[67]

James's waning popularity was further damaged by the outcome of the naval battle of Southwold Bay against the Dutch on 28 May 1672. Although James had shown great personal courage during the action and had to change ship on two occasions, the battle was inconclusive, and he was blamed for tactical naivety in allowing himself to be surprised by the Dutch. In June 1673 he laid down the office of Lord Admiral, partly in response to concerns on the part of Charles that he might recklessly endanger his life, but principally because the recently passed Test Act prohibited Roman Catholics from holding public office:

> They brought in a bill disabling all Papists from holding any employment, or place at Court; requiring all persons in publick trust to receive the Sacrament in a parish Church, and to carry an attested certificate of that, with witnesses to prove it, into Chancery, or the County Sessions; and there to make a declaration concerning Transubstantiation in full and positive words.[68]

James clearly could not comply with these provisions, and his response to requests that he might show some flexibility or dissimulation reveals clearly how his adherence to principle could shade into a faintly ludicrous self-importance: 'My Principles ... do not suffer me to Dissemble my Religion after that Manner; and I cannot obtain of my self to do Evil, that Good may come on't.'[69] As Charles would later remark to Schomberg, when he encouraged him to try to reconvert his brother, 'you know my brother long ago, that he is as stiff as a mule'.[70] James delivered his various commissions to the king, apparently in tears, while Charles received them without evident emotion. Nevertheless James retained influence over the navy, since the Admiralty was now put into a commission made up entirely of his creatures or associates.[71]

THE POPISH HEIR AND THE POPISH PLOT

James's conversion was politically momentous because of its implications for the succession. Charles had no legitimate children, and the health of his queen, Catherine of Braganza, who suffered from irregular and copious uterine bleeding, did not encourage hopes that any would be forthcoming. A series of miscarriages in the mid 1660s had resulted in the abandonment on Charles's part of attempts to father a legitimate child, while at the same time he shrank from more radical steps to remedy the situation, such as divorce and remarriage to a fertile wife. In December 1678 Charles admitted that although the queen was, he knew, 'a weak woman, and had some disagreeable humours', she was nevertheless not capable of wrongdoing, and given his own 'faultiness' towards her he thought it 'a horrid thing to abandon her'.[72] In the absence of a legitimate heir, James was the next in line to the throne. Although he had no surviving male children from his first marriage, his second, on 30 September 1673 to the youthful Mary Beatrice of Modena, increased the likelihood of a Catholic Stuart dynasty ruling over England for many years to come. The fact that at this time Modena was a client state of France did nothing to diminish the anxiety associated with this prospect. A series of miscarriages in the years following the marriage, and even an infant son born on 7 November 1677 (who, however, survived only five weeks), demonstrated that the new duchess was indeed fertile. As Hume would note: 'Popery, which had hitherto been only a hideous spectre, was now become a real ground of terror; being openly and zealously embraced by the heir to the crown, a prince of industry and enterprize.'[73]

There were two obvious remedies for the unpalatable prospect of a Catholic claimant as embodied in the steadily more unpopular James, and both were explored to varying degrees over the next decade. The first was to legitimize the Duke of Monmouth, the charismatic, popular, and – most importantly – Protestant son whom Charles had fathered on Lucy Walter in 1649. The second was to exclude James from the succession on the grounds of his religion. Both expedients involved tampering with the succession, a measure Charles regarded with deep aversion. In 1678 he said to Burnet, apropos the legitimation of Monmouth, that 'as well as he lov'd him, he had rather see him hanged' than agree to it.[74] Moreover in 1679 he would make a solemn declaration in Council 'that he was never married, nor contracted to that Duke's mother; nor to any other woman, except to his present Queen'.[75] On the other hand, and concerning the exclusion of James, Charles feared that to agree to such a step would set in motion a process that would change the nature of the English crown: 'he thought, if Acts of Exclusion were once begun, it would not be easy to stop them; but that upon any discontent at the next heir, they would be set on: religion was now the pretence: But other pretences would be found out, when there was need of them: This insensibly would change the nature of the *English* Monarchy: So that from being hereditary it would become elective.'[76] James would go even further in this line of analysis, and would see in Exclusion the first stirrings of a republican project to do away with the monarchy altogether.[77]

The prospect of a popish successor, which first crystallized in 1673, formed a watershed in domestic politics and dominated the final twelve years of Charles's reign, as Burnet would note:

Hitherto the reign of King Charles was pretty serene and calm at home. A Nation weary of a long civil war was not easily brought into jealousies and fears, which were the seeds of distraction, and might end in new confusions and troubles. But the Court had now given such broad intimations of an ill design, both on our religion and the civil constitution, that it was no more a jealousy: All was now open and barefaced.[78]

It was during the mid and late 1670s that the great fear of 'Popery and Arbitrary Government' took hold. As Marvell put it, in a pamphlet published in 1677 which captured the mood of much of the political nation: 'There has now for divers Years, a design been carried on, to change the Lawfull Government of England into an Absolute Tyranny, and to convert the established Protestant Religion into down-right Popery.'[79]

These fears were probably exaggerated. Charles used the eventual prospect of the reconversion of England to Roman Catholicism as bait to extract more money from Louis XIV, but there is little evidence to suggest that he was ever inclined seriously to pursue it. Nor did he wish to increase the powers of the crown (which were already, in theory at least, immense), but simply to be able to exercise the powers he considered rightfully his as king without interference. Burnet recorded a conversation which opens a window on to Charles's views about the scope and nature of kingly authority:

> The King said once to the Earl of *Essex*, as he told me, that he did not wish to be like a Grand Signior, with some mutes about him, and bags of bowstrings to strangle men, as he had a mind to it: But he did not think he was a King, as long as a company of fellows were looking into all his actions, and examining his Ministers, as well as his accounts.[80]

As naturally happens, Stuart loyalists responded to the agitation over popery and arbitrary government with an exaggeration of their own, seeing in the unrest a revival of the 1640s and 1650s: 'About the Year 1670, that *Republican Spirit*, which seemed extinct at the *Restauration*, began to kindle again from its Embers, and flame anew: the War which soon after was declared against the *Dutch*, gave the *Hydra* Faction an Opportunity to erect their Heads, and hiss again.'[81] Although there was indeed a republican fringe to this unease (as there would be again in 1688), it would be quite misleading to characterize either as republican – to do so would be to fall into the error of judgement which ensnared James himself whenever he pondered the motivation of those who opposed his measures. Those most deeply troubled by Stuart policies concerning the crown were not republicans (for whom the institution of monarchy was naturally not an object of affection), but rather loyal monarchists in whom attempts to enlarge the practical scope of the prerogative (whatever its apparent boundlessness in the rarefied zone of political theory) and to depart from customary practices aroused anguished disquiet. As Fox was to see so clearly, the two factions were on this occasion, as so often, seeking their own advantage, not trying dispassionately and accurately to describe their adversaries: 'Upon reviewing the two great parties of the nation, one observation occurs very forcibly, and that is, that the great strength of the Whigs consisted in their being able to brand their adversaries as favourers of Popery; that of the Tories (as far as their strength depended upon opinion, and not merely upon the power of the crown) in their finding colour to represent the Whigs as republicans.'[82]

In respect of James himself, the darkening national mood meant that he grew to be steadily more estranged from the

Church of England gentry whose deeply traditional political attitudes made them his natural supporters, but whose detestation of Roman Catholicism proved to be the stronger component in their opinions. Again, Fox would put his finger on the key point: 'Absolute power in civil matters, under the specious names of monarchy and prerogative, formed a most essential part of the Tory creed; but the order in which Church and King are placed in the favourite device of the party, is not accidental, and is well calculated to shew the genuine principles of such among them as are not corrupted by influence.'[83]

The marriage of James's elder daughter Mary to William of Orange on 4 November 1677 – a marriage so full of consequence for English history – was intended at least in part to take some of the edge off the popular resentment now attaching to James. So the Earl of Danby, one of the architects of the match, is reported to have explained to Charles when proposing it:

> The King said next, my brother will never consent to it. Lord *Danby* answered, perhaps not, unless the King took it upon him to command it: And he thought it was the Duke's interest to have it done, even more than the King's: All people were now possess'd of his being a Papist, and were very apprehensive of it: But if they saw his daughter given to one that was at the head of the Protestant interest, it would very much soften those apprehensions, when it did appear that his religion was only a personal thing, not to be derived to his children after him.[84]

However, these slight mitigations of the public mood were utterly dispelled by the astonishing events and revelations of the autumn of 1678.[85]

Three days before Michaelmas Israel Tonge – 'a very mean Divine . . . credulous and simple', a 'gardiner and a chymist, and . . . full of projects and notions' who 'had got some credit in *Cromwell*'s time: And that kept him poor' – called on Gilbert Burnet and told him of a Catholic plot to assassinate Charles and enthrone James, which he had learned of from one Titus Oates.[86] Tonge had apparently also been telling his story at court to anyone who would listen. Most of those who had heard it had dismissed it as groundless and unbelievable (a view shared by modern historians). But the more subtle minds of the time, such as George Savile, Marquess of Halifax, realized that the truth or falsehood of Tonge's story was as nothing in comparison with the explosiveness of how it might interact with the public mood. For given 'the suspicions all people had of the Duke's Religion . . . every discovery of that sort would raise a flame, which the Court would not be able to manage'.[87]

Oates's character and career to date ought not to have inspired confidence: 'He was the son of an Anabaptist teacher, who afterwards conformed, and got into orders, and took a benefice, as this his son did. He was proud and ill natured, haughty, but ignorant. He had been complained of for some very indecent expressions concerning the mysteries of the Christian Religion. He was once presented for perjury. But he got to be a Chaplain in one of the King's ships, from which he was dismiss'd upon complaint of some unnatural practices, not to be named.'[88] To this already substantial charge sheet might have been added expulsion from two Cambridge colleges.

But even self-evidently unreliable witnesses may be believed if the tales they tell chime with what those who hear them are disposed to accept; while those who see through their stories (for example, men such as Halifax) may nevertheless exploit the general credit such stories enjoy for their own benefit and in the pursuit of their political objectives. So it was to prove in the case of the Popish Plot:

> Oates's stories had such an effect because they appealed on different levels to every section of the nation, they confirmed assumptions about the Papists held by almost everyone, and they were coupled with the fear of absolutism and slavery.[89]

Oates's fluency under questioning, and the confiscation from the house of Edward Colman, secretary to Mary Beatrice (and allegedly to be made Secretary of State following the murder of Charles), of ciphered correspondence with important Catholic figures in Europe, including Louis XIV's confessors Jean Ferrier and François de la Chaise, Cardinal Howard, and the papal internuncio at Brussels, served only to stoke the flames. Some of these letters appeared to implicate James himself in plans for a change of monarch, and Colman claimed that they had all been written with James's approval. In one of the few truly shameful actions of his life, James denied that he had known of the correspondence. Colman was tried, convicted, and then hung, drawn and quartered – a punishment he endured with

1. Detail from *The Five Eldest Children of Charles I*, 1637, by Van Dyck (L–R: Mary, James, Charles). James has not yet been breeched.

2. James when Duke of York, *c*.1665, by Lely. The armour and baton evoke James's military character.

3. Battle of Lowestoft by van Diest. The painting shows James's moment of triumph, as the Dutch flagship burns in the right foreground.

4. James and Anne with daughters Mary and Anne by Lely. James's left arm rests proprietorially on a globe.

5. King James II by de Largillière, 1686. James wears the blue ribbon of the Order of the Garter, and the gold decoration on his armour incorporates both the lily of France and the rose of England, reflecting the Stuarts' claim to the throne of France.

6. Titus Oates in the pillory in New Palace Yard, 1687.

7. The seven bishops committed to the Tower in 1688. On their acquittal Burnet recorded that 'there were such shoutings, so long continued, and as it were echoed into the City, that all people were struck with it'.

8. 'a soft and happy gale of wind carried in the whole Fleet in four hours time into Torbay' – William III landing at Torbay on 5 November 1688.

9. Medal struck in 1788 commemorating the hundredth anniversary of the abdication of King James II. James is shown dropping the Great Seal into the Thames.

10. Battle of the Boyne, 1690. William's troops are just about to force the river and rout the Jacobite army. This is the moment that put an end to any serious prospect of James's restoration.

11. Mary of Modena and Prince James, c.1692, by Gennari. Prince James is about the same age in this picture as was his father in Plate 1.

12. Repository for James II's brain, at the former Scots College, Paris. The inscription on the plaque pays tribute to James's 'foi catholique, son courage dans l'adversité malgré la trahison, sa douceur et sa patience, [et] son élévation d'esprit'.

'much composedness and devotion'. Throughout he remained
true to James and refused to incriminate him, saying that it
was his own zeal in the cause of religion that had made him
too 'forward'.[90] To be bested in loyalty by the servant he
had betrayed must have been a mortifying experience for
James, not least because he had frequently deplored his
father's weakness (as he saw it) in not standing by men such
as Strafford and Laud.[91]

The consequences of the discovery of these letters, following on from Oates's allegations, were predictable, and
devastating:

> The whole town was all over enflamed with this discovery
> [Oates's testimony]. It consisted of so many particulars, that
> it was thought to be above invention. But when *Coleman*'s
> letters came to be read and examined, it got a great confirm-
> ation; since by these it appeared, that so many years before
> they thought the design for the converting the Nation, and
> rooting out the pestilent heresy that had reigned so long in
> these northern Kingdoms, was very near its being executed:
> Mention was oft made of the Duke's great zeal for it . . .[92]

So, in the popular mind, a Catholic plot to assassinate
Charles had indeed been planned; and the principle of *cui
bono* pointed irresistibly at his brother.

The mysterious murder of Sir Edmund Berry Godfrey,
the London JP before whom Oates had sworn to the truth
of his allegations on 6 September 1678, seemed to put the
matter beyond doubt. In the days before his death Godfrey
had regretted taking Oates's depositions, and gloomily

predicted that he would be 'knocked on the head'. He went missing on 12 October, and was found five days later, in strange circumstances which some interpreted as showing Catholic involvement in his murder:

> . . . his body was found in a ditch, about a mile out of the town, near St. *Pancras* Church. His sword was thrust thro' him. But no blood was on his clothes, or about him. His shoes were clean. His money was in his pocket. But nothing was about his neck. And a mark was all round it, an inch broad, which shewed he was strangled. His breast was likewise all over marked with bruises: And his neck was broken . . . There were many drops of white wax-lights on his breeches, which he never used himself. And since only persons of quality, or Priests, use those lights, this made all people conclude in whose hands he must have been.[93]

Although, as Hume would point out in the next century, there was no real evidence to connect Godfrey's death with Oates's allegations, the fevered atmosphere of London in the late 1670s was not propitious to measured scepticism: 'Parliaments were hot, and Juries were easy in this prosecution.'[94] The Whigs of the next century would be eager to dissociate themselves from the shameful witch-hunt that ensued, Fox going so far as to call the Popish Plot 'an indelible disgrace upon the English nation'.[95]

In the hope of calming men's minds and lowering the political temperature, Charles ordered James to leave the kingdom. On 3 March 1679 James and Mary Beatrice set sail for Holland and thence to Brussels, 'not without many tears shed by him at parting, tho' the King shed none'.[96]

THE EXCLUSION CRISIS

As it turned out James's period of enforced residence abroad did not have the desired effect. The fearsome image of a Catholic monarchy that the Popish Plot had raised in so lurid and so memorable a form was not easily to be sponged away. Moreover, it proved hard for people to put from their minds what the Popish Plot had also made alarmingly clear, that only the life of Charles stood between them and the dreaded prospect of Catholic kingship. The result was the Exclusion Crisis of 1679–81.[97]

There were three general elections between 1679 and 1681, and all three returned heavy majorities in the House of Commons for those who wished to exclude James from the succession. The Exclusionists, or Whigs as they came to be known, began from a conservative or defensive position. Their aim was to preserve what they believed to be the religious and political constitution which the English had inherited from their ancestors (to be sure, not without interruptions and upsets). To do this they proposed 'the excluding [James] simply, and making the succession to go on, as if he was dead, as the only mean that was easy and safe both for the Crown and the people: This was nothing but the disinheriting the next heir, which certainly the King and Parliament might do.'[98] But in order to pursue that ultimately conservative goal the Exclusionists were driven to measures that smacked of radicalism. In particular, the Exclusionist majority in the Commons found themselves repeatedly in conflict with both the king and the House of Lords, and this made them seem more given to constitutional innovation than was probably the case.[99]

The principal Exclusionist was Anthony Ashley Cooper, later Earl of Shaftesbury, who was immortalized and vilified for posterity by Dryden in the character of Achitophel:

> For close designs and crooked counsels fit,
> Sagacious, bold, and turbulent of wit;
> Restless, unfixed in principles and place,
> In power unpleased, impatient of disgrace.
> A fiery soul, which working out its way
> Fretted the pigmy body to decay,
> And o'erinformed the tenement of clay.
> A daring pilot in extremity:
> Pleased with the danger, when the waves went high
> He sought the storms; but for a calm unfit
> Would steer too nigh the sands to boast his wit.[100]

Shaftesbury's loyalties were undeniably volatile. During the Civil War Sir Anthony Ashley Cooper (as he then was) had hesitated over which side to join. In the summer of 1643 he had raised troops for the Royalists, but the following year he had resigned his commissions under the king and had associated himself with the Parliamentarians (as he said because he realized that Charles I's policies would be 'destructive to religion and the state').[101] Thereafter Cooper served on the Parliamentarian side throughout the 1640s, and under Cromwell he had sat on the Council of State. In the

mid 1650s, however, Cooper had separated himself from
Cromwell, and had begun to receive overtures from the
exiled Stuart court. He did not respond encouragingly until
English politics had reached a crisis of confusion in the
early months of 1660. At this stage Cooper was clearly per-
ceived to be acceptable to the exiled court, since he was one
of the twelve Members of the House of Commons chosen
to travel to the Hague and invite Charles II to return to
England.

On the Restoration Cooper's chequered past seemed to be
forgotten and forgiven. He had been pardoned for his actions
during the Civil War, becoming a member of the Privy
Council and shortly afterwards Chancellor of the Exchequer
and Under-Treasurer. He had been one of the 'Cabal' of
five ministers who shouldered the burden of administration
from 1668 to 1673, and in 1672 he was ennobled as Earl of
Shaftesbury and subsequently became Lord Chancellor.

However, these high offices and favours had not made
Shaftesbury compliant on the question of the succession: a
strong aversion to Roman Catholicism is a thread of consist-
ency running through his various reversals and contortions
of allegiance. In 1673 he had orchestrated parliamentary
manoeuvres to prevent the consummation of James's marriage with Mary Beatrice, and when that failed he had
badgered Charles to divorce the queen and take a new, fertile, wife. James had been outraged by these actions, and had
asked Charles to dismiss Shaftesbury, which he had done
on 9 November.

Yet, although he had fallen from office, Shaftesbury was
naturally still a Member of Parliament with a seat in the

House of Lords, and for the next four years he would use his position there to issue warnings concerning the dangers of popery. In 1675 he had published an alarmist pamphlet claiming that since the Restoration an unholy alliance of High Church and old Cavalier interests had been plotting to transform the government into a despotism 'not bounded or limited by humane Laws'.[102] He had also spoken out passionately against the revival of doctrines of divine right monarchy: themes which he had reprised in a celebrated speech in the Lords on 25 March 1679. With such a public profile Shaftesbury naturally became a focus for MPs opposed to the measures of the court and other disaffected elements. Although Shaftesbury was not, in any sense that we would recognize, the leader of a party, he nevertheless was very influential in the direction of attempts during the following three years to nullify the threat of a Catholic succession by excluding James from the throne, even going so far in the summer of 1680 as to present James to the grand jury of Middlesex as a popish recusant.

At the heart of the arguments for Exclusion was a particular conception of the ends and nature of human government: 'Government was appointed for those that were to be governed, and not for the sake of Governors themselves: Therefore all things relating to it were to be measured by the publick interest, and the safety of the people.'[103] These notions are not too far removed from our modern ideas of government, and so it is tempting for us to regard them as easy and natural. But in 1679, they would have seemed strange and new. Men were then for the most part more comfortable with an idea that now to us seems very outlandish, namely that the state was a sacral body ordained by God, and that questions of secular utility had to yield to considerations of divine ordination: 'Law could not alter what God had settled.'[104] The project of Exclusion challenged entrenched beliefs about the nature of society, its ends and government, and unsurprisingly therefore it proved to be both unsuccessful and bitterly divisive. The successive pieces of legislation proposed by the Exclusionists passed the Commons but failed to become law; and Charles's gift for delay and procrastination meant that eventually the energies raised by Shaftesbury and his associates were dissipated, and the Whigs defeated. Shaftesbury would flee to the Low Countries in 1682, arriving in Amsterdam just in time to die, as Burnet remarked.[105] Even the numerous executions in the wake of the Popish Plot, which had extended as late as 1679, eventually had the effect of dampening the public agitation:

> It was like the letting blood (as one observed) which abates a fever. Every execution, like a new bleeding, abated the heat that the Nation was in; and threw us into a cold deadness, which was like to prove fatal to us.[106]

Although they were unable to secure their main objective, the Exclusionists did however make a lasting impact in the realm of political tactics:

> The first Whigs were, and had to be, a party, something more highly organized and disciplined than a mere alliance or coalition of small and autonomous groups. They possessed, and required, organization in both Parliament and country,

effective discipline, and a wide popular appeal, stimulated and maintained by a large-scale propaganda machine.[107]

This new thoroughness and co-ordination was evident both within Parliament, where the Whigs had used their sequence of majorities to harass the Tories and attack the Church;[108] and also out of doors in prototypical political campaigning. As part of this effort to mould public opinion Shaftesbury had stopped at nothing, not even at making an instrument out of Charles's illegitimate son:

> he [Monmouth] gave himself fatally up to the Lord *Shaftsbury*'s conduct, who put him on all the methods imaginable to make himself popular. He went round many parts of *England*, pretending it was for hunting and horse matches, many thousands coming together in most places to see him: So that this looked like the mustering up the force of the party: But it really weakned it: Many grew jealous of the design, and fancied here was a new civil war to be raised. Upon this they joined in with the Duke's party. Lord *Shaftsbury* set also on foot petitions for a Parliament, in order to the securing the King's person, and the Protestant Religion. These were carried about and signed in many places ... And many well meaning men began to dislike those practices, and to apprehend that a change of government was designed.[109]

Notwithstanding the failure of this audacious experiment to influence the temper of the people, the extraordinary electoral success achieved by the Whigs in the years 1679–81, and the means whereby that success had been secured, would not be forgotten by James and his advisers after his accession in 1685: 'The lesson of the Exclusion Crisis was clear; control over the boroughs was the prerequisite of effective control over Parliament. Consequently, municipal affairs became as central an issue in English politics as they were in the struggles for power in contemporary Holland.'[110]

JAMES IN EXILE

Brussels was familiar to James from twenty years earlier, but he found little to amuse him there now. He spent his time hunting, until Charles fell ill in August 1679 'of an intermitting fever'.[111] The symptoms seemed so alarming that James was advised to come to England at once, travelling in disguise via Calais. By the time he arrived in London on 2 September Charles had recovered, and furthermore had determined that James should once again be sent out of England. The destination this time, however, was Scotland, where James would serve as Charles's High Commissioner from October 1679 until March 1682.

In the months preceding James's arrival Scotland had been disturbed by resistance to the severe administration of the Duke of Lauderdale. The Nonconformists had been vigorously repressed, and this had led to the open and armed rebellion of the Cameronians at Bothwell Bridge. James was to acquire a reputation for severity in Scotland, based in large measure on Burnet's report that he had observed prisoners being tortured 'with an unmoved indifference, and with an attention, as if he had been to look on some curious experiment. This gave a terrible idea of him to all that observed it, as of a man that had no bowels nor humanity in him.'[112] But it would be misleading to extrapolate from that to the character of James's administration in Scotland as a whole, which seems not to have been a 'fiery persecution'.[113] Burnet paints instead an administration whose attention to its own interest encouraged it down the paths of moderation: 'things were so gently carried, that there was no cause of complaint. It was visibly his interest to make that Nation sure to him, and to give them such an essay of his government, as might dissipate all the hard thoughts of him with which the world was possessed ... And so, considering how much that Nation was set against his Religion, he made a greater progress in gaining upon them than was expected.'[114] Notwithstanding this suaveness of manner, however, business was driven on at a smart pace. James tended to put bills on a very short debate to the vote, and tended always to prevail when he did so.[115] There is surely a trace here of high-handedness, of an autocratic drive which would express itself more openly if it could. It is therefore particularly remarkable that when James left Scotland, having been given permission by Charles to return to court permanently in March 1682, the Scottish bishops wrote to Archbishop Sancroft to praise 'in a very high strain' James's affection to the Church, and insisted on the care he had taken of it.[116] On his return, all seemed set fair. He was 'highly complimented by all, and seemed to have overcome all difficulties'.[117]

THE 'TORY REVENGE'

The agitation surrounding Exclusion had not only been extremely divisive. It had also bred in the hearts of the Anglican gentry a willingness to tolerate, in some perhaps even a desire to pursue, strong measures to suppress those whom they feared might involve the nation in another civil war. James would take a lead in the implementation of these measures, particularly during the last two years of Charles's reign, when he seemed to have the government 'wholly in his hands':

> *Scotland* was so entirely in his dependance, that the King would seldom ask what the papers imported, which the Duke brought to be signed by him. In *England*, the application and dependance was visibly on the Duke. The King had scarce company about him to entertain him, when the Duke's levees and couchees were so crouded, that the antichambers were full. The King walked about with a small train of the necessary attendants, when the Duke had a vast following: Which drew a lively reflection from *Waller* the celebrated wit. He said, the House of Commons had resolved that the Duke should not reign after the King's death: But the King in opposition to them was resolved that he should reign even during his life.[118]

Yet the so-called 'Tory Revenge' was carried forward on a number of fronts, not all of them equally agreeable to James.

In the first place, the effective use the Whigs had made of their parliamentary majorities between 1679 and 1681 had not been forgotten; in particular, it had been noted that many boroughs had returned Whigs to the House of Commons, and so had contributed strongly to the resulting Exclusionist majorities. In order to reverse this situation and to hand over political control of as many boroughs as possible to the Tories, the policy known as *quo warranto* was devised:[119]

> The Cities and Boroughs of *England* were invited, and prevailed on, to demonstrate their loyalty, by surrendring up their Charters, and taking new ones modelled as the Court thought fit.[120]

The mechanism of the policy was to call in a borough's charter and then to reissue it, the new charter, however, bestowing greatly enlarged powers on the crown to nominate officials and to veto elections: and 'the King reserved a power to himself to turn out magistrates at his pleasure'.[121] Occasionally the franchise of a borough would also be more closely restricted in order the better to procure the election of a supporter of the court: 'the election of the members was taken out of the hands of the inhabitants, and restrained to the Corporation-men, all those being left out who were not acceptable at Court'.[122] The result was that the court now had much greater influence than before over the composition of the House of Commons. Secondly, the laws against Roman Catholics and Dissenters began to be enforced much more strictly. James sat on a commission for ecclesiastical appointments, and working in harness with his first wife's brother, the Earl of Rochester, he set about ensuring that the bench of bishops was populated by High Churchmen.

At the same time James embarked upon some experiments in the practice of absolutism on the far side of the Atlantic. In 1664 Charles had granted New Netherland to James, and after the conclusion of the Third Dutch War in 1674 James had entered into possession of the proprietary colony which was then renamed in his honour New York. James ruled the colony through his deputy governor, Richard Nicholls. Rule was enforced by a strong garrison, and there were no forms of popular democracy. It was only a desire to increase taxation revenue that induced James to give permission for an assembly, which met for the first time in October 1683. In 1686 James would extend his sway to include Massachusetts, Connecticut, New Hampshire and Rhode Island, eventually unifying these territories with New York and New Jersey into a single crown colony. Under its governor, Sir Edmund Andros, a repressive regime was established with arbitrary imprisonment, a standing army and censorship of the press. In respect of religion, James introduced freedom of worship, which naturally was as unwelcome to the Puritan bigots of New England as the instruments of secular absolutism that had been instituted alongside it.

It was the Rye House Plot of June 1683, and its aftermath, which further tightened James's grip on power in England. The essence of the plot (which according to Burnet was nothing but loose talk from an old Cromwellian named Rumbold) was to assassinate Charles and James as they returned to London from Newmarket:

> ... he had a farm near *Hodsden* in the way to *New-Market*: And there was a moat cast round his house, thro' which the King sometimes past in his way thither. He said, once the coach went thro' quite alone, without any of the guards about it; and that, if he had laid any thing cross the way to have stopt the coach but a minute, he could have shot them both, and have rode away thro' grounds that he knew so well that it should not have been possible to have followed him.[123]

When the conspiracy came to light and the plotters were arrested, it emerged that various peers either were, or could be made to seem, implicated in it. These included the Duke of Monmouth, Algernon Sidney, Lord Russell and the Earl of Essex. Monmouth was pardoned, Sidney and Russell executed, and Essex died in suspicious circumstances while imprisoned in the Tower – murder made to appear like suicide was the popular suspicion.

An important consequence of the Rye House Plot was that James's political position was greatly strengthened. He was restored to the Cabinet council in June 1683; in May 1684 he was reinstated as Lord Admiral (the provisions of the Test Act thereby being set aside, in his case); and he resumed the direction of naval affairs. In the same month he returned to the Privy Council. He also acquired new and important allies at court. The Earl of Sunderland had been a supporter of Exclusion, but he now associated himself with James, as did Charles's mistress, the Duchess of

Portsmouth. Meanwhile, James's enemies and rivals were suffering. Monmouth, pardoned but unforgiven, withdrew himself to the Low Countries in 1684. There he was entertained by William of Orange who believed, probably mistakenly, that in so doing he would be pleasing Charles. At court James's principal adversary, Halifax, began to lose influence. Emboldened by these developments, James began to adopt a more openly pro-Catholic policy, particularly in Ireland.

The decisive turn of events came in February 1685, when Charles was taken ill while shaving:

> ... the King, who seemed all the while to be in great confusion, fell down all of a sudden in a fit like an apoplexy: He looked black, and his eyes turned in his head.[124]

He had suffered a severe stroke. Autopsy revealed that 'so many of the small veins of the brain were burst, that the brain was in great disorder, and no judgment could be made concerning it'.[125] James was at Charles's bedside during the crisis, and arranged for him to receive the Sacraments from a Catholic priest, John Huddleston, who as it happens had helped Charles escape from the Battle of Worcester in 1650. Huddleston 'made the King go thro' some acts of contrition, and, after such a confession as he could then make, he gave him absolution and the other Sacraments. The hostie stuck in his throat: ... He also gave him extream Unction. All must have been performed very superficially, since it was so soon ended. But the King seemed to be at great ease upon it. It was given out, that the King said to *Hudleston*, that he had saved him twice, first his body, and now his soul . . .'[126]

There were, inevitably, suspicions of poison. Charles, it was said, had been on the point of agreeing to exclude James from the succession, and perhaps of taking the further step of legitimizing Monmouth. Knowing of these imminent moves from the confessor of the Duchess of Portsmouth, the Catholics had acted ruthlessly to preserve the succession of their co-religionist, James. Some did not hesitate afterwards to implicate even James himself in this supposed assassination.[127] But in the days following Charles's death all was quiet, as Sir John Reresby recalled of the public response in York to the proclamation of James as king: 'All this was transacted with all imaginable Tokens of Peace and Joy; not only in *York* itself, but afterwards throughout the whole County, and, indeed, the whole Kingdom.'[128]

3
King of England, Scotland and Ireland

EARLY CHALLENGES AND SUCCESSES

At the first meeting of the Privy Council following his accession James began by touching on the suspicions which had been entertained of his character and policies when Duke of York, and the fear that when he became king he would introduce popery and arbitrary government to England. While he admitted that he intended to make full use of the royal prerogative, he nevertheless volunteered a number of reassurances in respect of law, of property and of religion:

> I shall make it my endeavour to preserve this government both in church and state as it is by law established. I know the principles of the Church of England are for monarchy and the members of it have shown themselves good and loyal subjects; therefore I shall always take care to defend and support it. I know too that the laws of England are sufficient to make the king as great a monarch as I can wish; and as I shall never depart from the rights and prerogative of the crown, so I shall never invade any man's property.[1]

These undertakings soon became generally known, since James agreed to have this short speech published. It 'gave great content to those who believed that he would stick to the promises made in it. And those few, who did not believe it, yet durst not seem to doubt of it.'[2] It was apparently much referred to from the pulpit, where it was praised as providing a security greater than could arise from any mere law. However, the early months of James's reign were also disfigured by some acts of petty retribution, including that against Titus Oates, for whom a cruel and unusual punishment was specifically devised:

> So he was condemned to have his Priestly habit taken from him, to be a prisoner for life, to be set on the pillory in all the publick places of the City, and ever after that to be set on the pillory four times a year, and to be whipt by the common hangman from *Aldgate* to *Newgate* one day, and the next from *Newgate* to *Tyburn*; which was executed with so much rigour, that his back seemed to be all over flead ... Yet he, who was an original in all things, bore this with a constancy that amazed all those who saw it. So that this treatment did rather raise his reputation, than sink it.[3]

The harsh treatment of Oates and its paradoxical effect on public opinion accurately set the keynote for James's reign. The measures on which the new king would rely to cement and proclaim his authority in the event served only to undermine and weaken it.

As might have been expected, there were changes in the royal household. Halifax was made Lord President of the

Council, but real power lay elsewhere. James's two brothers-in-law, the Earl of Rochester and the Earl of Clarendon, were made respectively Lord Treasurer and Lord Privy Seal. Although they were both staunch members of the Church of England, James clearly believed that they could be trusted implicitly. More surprising was the rise of the Earl of Sunderland.[4] Like Halifax, Sunderland had voted for Exclusion. But he had since insinuated himself into the confidence of the queen, and soon became the dominant figure in James's administration. In private life a reckless gambler, Sunderland viewed politics in a similar light. He had no settled policies or durable commitments, just as a gambler has no deeper attachment to red than to black, or to spades than to clubs. His sole objective seems to have been to survive, if possible to thrive, and this dictated a particular stance towards the throne: 'He wondered anybody would be so silly as to dispute with kings; for if they would not take good advice there was no way of dealing with them, but by running into their measures till they had ruined themselves.'[5] This lack of challenge to James's wishes would eventually give rise to a paranoid Jacobite interpretation of Sunderland's conduct, namely that he was secretly in the counsels of William of Orange, and had encouraged James in policies which he knew would prove ruinous. So thought James's natural son, the Duke of Berwick:

> It is true, that on several occasions, perhaps too little circum-spection had been used [in the pursuit of the King's business], which had given rise to false ideas: but it is equally certain, that, independent of the indiscreet zeal of the catholics, the

Earl of Sunderland had contributed to this more than any
other person; and that, with a view of ruining the King, and
of paving the way for the enterprizes of the Prince of Orange,
who had long ago gained him over.[6]

Modern historians have concluded otherwise. Sunderland
was certainly this duplicitous, but he was neither so deep
nor so accomplished. His administration is more accurately
viewed as a series of increasingly desperate improvisations.

James's first (and only) parliament met from February to
November 1685. In the elections leading up to it the remodelling of the boroughs achieved during the previous reign
by the policy of *quo warranto* proved their value. As James
remarked with satisfaction when the returns were all in,
'there were not above forty members, but such as he himself
wished for'.[7] The satisfaction in Whitehall, however, was
not universally shared:

This gave all thinking men a melancholy prospect. England
now seemed lost, unless some happy accident should save it.
All people saw the way for packing a Parliament now laid
open. A new set of Charters and Corporation-men, if those
now named should not continue to be still as compliant as
they were at present, was a certain remedy, to which recourse
might be easily had. The Boroughs of England saw their priv-
ileges now wrested out of their hands, and that their elections,
which had made them so considerable before, were hereafter
to be made as the Court should direct: So that from hence-
forth little regard would be had to them; and the usual

practices in courting, or rather in corrupting them, would be no longer pursued.[8]

In respect of finance, this new parliament did all that James could have asked, granting him a large revenue for life, rather than for only a period of years, by which means they would have retained some influence. In so doing they followed James's imperious advice to them, that to grant a temporary revenue would be 'a very improper method to take with me'.[9] But in other respects they showed some backbone. They resisted court-sponsored measures to expand the scope of treason to include words as well as deeds. Furthermore, and to James's annoyance, they stood up for the defence of the Church against both Roman Catholicism and dissent.

The overall mood of loyalty in the nation was strengthened by two abortive uprisings in the months following James's accession. In Scotland, the Earl of Argyll had landed with a handful of adherents, and had raised the banner of rebellion. He managed to recruit some 2,500 men, but he was soon captured by the militia, brought to Edinburgh, and executed. More serious was the landing of the Duke of Monmouth on 11 June at Lyme in Dorset. He quickly gathered an army of some 2,000 men, and published a pungently Whiggish manifesto, in which he referred to James as only Duke of York; called him a traitor, an assassin, a tyrant and a popish usurper; and accused him of setting the fire of London, of the murders of Sir Edmund Berry Godfrey and the Earl of Essex, and of the poisoning of Charles II. On

5 July Monmouth attempted a night attack on the army James had sent against him, which was negligently encamped at Sedgemoor. It was a bold move, but through a combination of mischance and inexperience among Monmouth's officers it miscarried. Three days later Monmouth was captured and taken to London, where he pleaded with James for his life, but to no avail. He was beheaded in a slovenly and incompetent manner on 15 July 1685.

In the event, neither of these uprisings posed a serious military or political challenge to James. But the policies James pursued in their aftermath did have important consequences. In the first place, in the West Country, where Monmouth had gathered his support, James gave his approval to vicious reprisals, initially by the army, subsequently by means of the law and the 'Bloody Assizes' conducted by the notorious Judge Jeffreys. Secondly, because the militia had performed poorly at the outset of the campaign against Monmouth, James decided to build up his standing forces. As part of this he decided to include Catholics amongst the officer corps, contrary to the provisions of the Test Act:

The King told them [Parliament] how happy his forces had been in reducing a dangerous rebellion, in which it had appeared, how weak and insignificant the Militia was: And therefore he saw the necessity of keeping up an Army for all their security. He had put some in commission, of whose loyalty he was well assured: And they had served him so well, that he would not put that affront on them, and on himself, to turn them out.[10]

James's determination on these two points – raising and maintaining a standing army, and granting dispensations from the Test Act to Roman Catholic officers – touched his subjects where they were most wincingly tender. Moreover, recent events in France had roused in England fears of a general European crisis in Protestantism. Louis XIV had begun persecuting his Protestant subjects (or Huguenots) by means of *dragonnades*, in which soldiers were billeted on Protestant families and intimidated them with violence. He had proceeded in 1685 to revoke the Edict of Nantes, under which the Huguenots had enjoyed a measure of toleration; and many of the resulting refugees had sought asylum in England. When James tried to go one step further and have the Test Acts repealed, Parliament voted for an address to the throne, urging the king to maintain the laws of the realm, and in particular the Test Acts. Greatly displeased, James prorogued Parliament on 20 November 1685.

During the following months James tried to change the minds of those who had opposed the repeal of the Test Acts, summoning them for private conversations in his closet (a practice which gave rise to the term 'closeting'). The resistance to James's pressure by Admiral Herbert, a well-known rake and debauchee, made a particular impression:

Admiral *Herbert*, being pressed by the King to promise that he would vote the repeal of the Test, answered the King very plainly, that he could not do it either in honour nor conscience. The King said, he knew he was a man of honour, but the rest of his life did not look like a man that had great regard to conscience. He answered boldly, he had his faults, but they were such, that other people, who talked more of conscience, were guilty of the like. He was indeed a man abandoned to luxury and vice. But, tho' he was poor, and had much to lose, having places to the value of 4000 *l.* a year, he chose to lose them all rather than comply.[11]

Herbert's sturdy resistance and James's response to it carried two implications: one for James, the other for his people. The latter might now see that in the eyes of the king past service would count for nothing unless accompanied by a willingness to acquiesce in the repeal of the Test Acts. The king, however, might have read in Herbert's firmness an indication of the likely response of many of his other subjects to any attempts by the crown to undermine the constitutional position of the Church of England.

When James found that few were prepared to revise their position concerning repeal of the Tests, he decided to dissolve Parliament. It was a rash move: 'he threw off a body of men that were in all other respects sure to him, and that would have accepted a very moderate satisfaction from him at any time. And indeed in all England it would not have been easy to have found five hundred men, so weak, so poor, and so devoted to the Court, as these were.'[12] So James began the ruinous dismantling of the strongest supports of his own regime.

LEGAL AND RELIGIOUS TENSIONS

On ascending the throne James had two broad objectives: one religious, the other political. In the first place, he wanted to remove the legal penalties that applied to Roman Catholicism, and to place his co-religionists on an equal footing with members of the Church of England. Eventually this led him also to show a degree of favour to the Dissenters. Previously he had been quick to stigmatize religious Nonconformists as covert republicans, incorrigibly disaffected towards monarchy. Now he saw them in a gentler light, as peaceable subjects who should be left to pursue the religious path they had chosen without molestation:

> The maxim that the King set up, and about which he entertained all that were about him, was, the great happiness of an universal toleration. On this the King used to enlarge in a great variety of topicks. He said, nothing was more reasonable, more christian, and more politick: And he reflected much on the Church of *England* for the severities with which Dissenters had been treated.[13]

Beyond toleration, however, lay a much larger aspiration, namely the reconversion of England to Roman Catholicism. This, James would say, he was 'resolved to bring about, or to die a Martyr in endeavouring it; and . . . he would rather suffer death for carrying on that, than live ever so long and happy without attempting it'.[14] His son-in-law, William of Orange, foresaw the perils of pursuing this goal: 'the Roman religion could not become dominant without the King's breaking the laws and his own promises and without (he feared) one day causing disorders which would imperil the monarchy'.[15] But James gave no sign of wanting to achieve the conversion of England by force. His – perhaps naive – hope was that once English men and women had become accustomed to Roman Catholicism, large numbers of them would spontaneously convert: 'James II himself even thought that not only was the Church of England sustained by the state, but that without the proscription of popery the kingdom could become Catholic within two years.'[16] The repeal of the Tests was to be a crucial step in the attainment of this goal.

Secondly, James wanted at the very least to maintain the rights and powers of the crown, and he wished also to make the crown a more efficient and more effective element in the constitution. His reign would be notable for moves towards a modernized, centralized bureaucracy.[17] These religious and political objectives would both need to be secured to some degree by means of law. The repeal of the Tests would be self-evidently a legal measure. At the same time, James's determination to employ his co-religionists in positions of trust, as men loyal to him on whom he could rely, committed him to the unusually vigorous exercise of part of the royal prerogative and to dispensing with the provisions of the Test Acts in their cases (the Declaration of Indulgence of 1687 would go so far in defence of this policy as to argue that it was against the law of nature for a king to be deprived of the service of any of his subjects). No one doubted that the crown did have a dispensing power, so in acting as he did James was in one sense staying within the bounds of law. What increasing numbers of people came gradually to feel, however, was that James's reliance on the dispensing power to achieve his objectives involved its application to cases it was never intended to meet – or, at least, where it had not customarily been used. However, and despite what Macaulay would say about them a century and a half later, James's goals were neither ridiculous nor backward-looking – indeed, quite the reverse.

In James's other kingdoms of Scotland and Ireland similar religious and political objectives were pursued, albeit with slight variations of approach and success as a result of the very different confessional composition of those two kingdoms. In Scotland (where he ruled as James VII) the great majority of the population were Presbyterian. James had entrusted the government of this kingdom to the Drummond brothers, the Lords Melfort and Perth, who were both converts to Catholicism. Public order was rendered more secure, but the policy of the promotion of Catholicism made little headway among the Scots, most of whom were unmoved by inducements and unafraid of punishments. Eventually the Drummond brothers seem to have quietly abandoned attempts to advance Catholicism, and concentrated instead on exploiting their offices to line their pockets.

In Ireland the dominant figure was an old and trusted associate of James, Richard Talbot, later Earl of Tyrconnell. The population of Ireland comprised three elements: the old, Catholic, Irish; the old, Catholic, English; and the new, Protestant, English, who had settled there relatively recently and who had been greatly favoured in the government of the island. The political turmoil of the mid seventeenth century had left a particularly deep mark on this kingdom, a telling indicator of which is the volatility of landholding as measured against religious confession. In 1641, Catholics held 60 per cent of Irish land. In 1660, after the expropriations following Cromwell's conquest, they held 9 per cent; 1662 and the Act of Settlement had seen a partial unwinding of that tendency, and Catholic landholding had risen to 20 per cent – which was of course still a long way short of its pre-1641 level. Tyrconnell was of old English stock, and he was determined to undo the reversals suffered by his fraction of the population. Accordingly he began an energetic remodelling of the institutions of the kingdom, particularly the army, in the Catholic interest. Although Tyrconnell was close to James, his motives were interestingly complex. He may have felt a deeper attachment to his homeland than to his monarch. Certainly he was careful to ensure that the steps he took might still benefit Ireland, should James's cause falter.

In England, an early flashpoint arose in the summer of 1686 when John Sharp, the Rector of St Giles-in-the-Fields, preached a sermon which included criticism of Roman Catholicism, and at which the court took offence. On 17 June James ordered Henry Compton, the Bishop of London, to suspend Sharp. Compton had a track record of resisting what he saw as James's encroachments. Although – perhaps, because – as Dean of the Chapels Royal Compton had in the past assumed some responsibility for the education of James's daughters, Mary and Anne, the two men had clashed during the reign of Charles II. James had opposed Compton's elevation to the bishopric of London. For his part, in the wake of the Popish Plot Compton had ordered the arrest of Roman Catholics who were known to take Mass in the private chapels of ambassadors. Since James's accession Compton had spoken in the House of Lords criticizing James's use of his dispensing power to make possible the employment of Roman Catholic officers, contrary to the Test Act. Such a flouting of the law, he had argued, imperilled the whole constitution.

Compton's response to James's order for Sharp's suspension was measured, outwardly deferential, but also inwardly firm:

> The Bishop answered, that he had no power to proceed in such a summary way: But, if an accusation were brought into his Court in a regular way, he would proceed to such a censure as could be warranted by the Ecclesiastical law . . .[18]

James decided to treat this resistance to his wishes as contempt, rather than adherence to law and due process, and so on 9 August he ordered Compton to be summoned before a new body that had been formed to give effect to the crown's religious policy, the Ecclesiastical Commission. By creating this commission James had defied the tendency of earlier legislation:

> The Act that put down the High Commission in the year 1640 had provided by a clause, as full as could be conceived, that no Court should be ever set up for those matters, besides

the ordinary Ecclesiastical Courts. Yet in contempt of that a Court was erected, with full power to proceed in a summary and arbitrary way in all Ecclesiastical matters, without limitations to any rule of law in their proceedings. This stretch of the supremacy, so contrary to law, was assumed by a King, whose religion made him condemn all that supremacy that the law had vested in the Crown.[19]

Compton was summoned before this body. His defence was that he had obeyed the king so far as he legally could. As he explained, he could not lay an ecclesiastical censure on any of his clergy without a process, and articles, and the production of proof or evidence. Unimpressed by this defence, or at least not daring to be persuaded by it, the commission voted to suspend Compton, although they did not make any attempt to confiscate or withhold his revenues. To do so would have been to meddle with freehold property, and this would have embroiled James in a much more serious legal battle where the odds were not so heavily in his favour (as he would discover later in his clash with the fellows of Magdalen College, Oxford).

The legal aspect of these religious struggles centred on that part of the royal prerogative known as the dispensing power, namely the king's right to abrogate a law when particular circumstances justified it. Implicit in its traditional use was the understanding that this power would be used infrequently. In particular, people did not expect it to be used systematically as a way of circumventing the regular way of removing a legal penalty, namely repeal by Act of Parliament. Moreover, the use of the prerogative in religious matters had been declared unconstitutional in 1663 and 1673. But now James had begun to use his dispensing power in just such a systematic way, and in relation to questions of religion, to the point where it seemed to be in effect broadening into something much more alarming and potentially despotic: that is to say, a power to suspend the operation of a law.

James sought to have his innovative use of this part of his prerogative clarified in his favour by means of a collusive action in the courts. Sir Edward Hales was a Catholic who held an army commission, and who therefore could not conform to the Test Act. However, Hales claimed that he had a dispensation from James releasing him from the obligation to take communion in the Church of England. Hales's coachman was set up to inform against his master, his inducement being the £500 reward for doing so. When the case was brought the prosecution were said to have argued with deliberate weakness, while the twelve judges of the common law courts who heard the case had been carefully selected to bring in the desired verdict. Unsurprisingly, all but one upheld the arguments used by the defence to vindicate the use of the dispensing power in matters of religion, maintaining:

> that the government of *England* was entirely in the King: That the Crown was an Imperial Crown, the importance of which was, that it was absolute: All penal laws were powers lodged in the Crown to enable the King to force the execution of the law, but were not bars to limit or bind up the King's power: The King could pardon all offences against the

law, and forgive the penalties: And why could he not as well dispense with them?[20]

The theoretical point was thus gained. But, as James would eventually discover, in politics theory has far less agency than opinion. No matter what judgment had been given in this particular case, the people clearly understood that repeated exercise of the dispensing power might be tantamount to the dissolution of the whole government.

As part of his general remodelling of the great institutions of the kingdom James turned next to the universities, which at this time were monopolies of the Church of England. James was determined to open their gates to Roman Catholics. Cambridge was ordered to confer a degree on a Benedictine monk, but when they refused the matter was dropped. A more grave and determined effort was made in Oxford. Here perhaps it was believed, on the basis of the fawning addresses the University had recently offered to James, that less resistance would be encountered. The President of Magdalen having died, on 5 April 1687 James wrote to the fellows and ordered them to elect Anthony Farmer, 'an ignorant and vitious person' who in various ways did not meet the requirements laid down in the college statutes for a President.[21] The fellows explained the reasons why Farmer was ineligible and elected in his stead one of their own number, John Hough. Baffled in his wish to see Farmer elected, James now insisted that the fellows of Magdalen elect Samuel Parker, the Bishop of Oxford. The fellows, however, were not to be intimidated:

They excused themselves, since they were bound by their oaths to maintain their statutes: And by these, an election being once made and confirmed, they could not proceed to a new choice, till the former was annulled in some Court of law: Church benefices and College preferments were freeholds, and could only be judged in a Court of Record: And, since the King was now talking so much of liberty of conscience, it was said, that the forcing men to act against their oaths, seemed not to agree with those professions.[22]

James was infuriated and resolved on yet stronger measures. He came to Oxford, harangued the fellows, made forcible entry into the President's lodgings so that Parker might be put in possession, and ejected all that would not submit to their new head of house.

The fellows, however, had touched on the vital point when they had mentioned that their fellowships were freeholds, for this meant that the deprivation they had suffered at James's hands was little more than an open act of robbery. By these proceedings James had showed that he either set little store by the undertaking he had given on his accession, that he would 'never invade any man's property', or that he did not understand it. At the same time, his persecution of the fellows of Magdalen completed the rupture with the Church of England that had been deepening since the proroguing of Parliament in November 1685:

Now the King broke with the Church of *England*. And, as he was apt to go warmly upon every provocation, he gave himself such liberties in discourse upon that subject, that it was plain, all the services they had done him, both in opposing Exclusion, and upon his first accession to the Crown, were forgot. Agents were now found out, to go among the Dissenters, to persuade them to accept of the favour the King intended them, and to concur with him in his designs.[23]

James now took advice from only a small group of Catholic ultras: 'he had both Priests and flatterers about him, that were still pushing him forward'.[24] The moderating influence of men such as Clarendon and Rochester, loyal both to James and to the Church of England, had been lost when they had been dismissed. Lost, too, had been the information such important men could have given James about popular sentiment in their localities. The combination of James's natural stubbornness and the absence of the occasional challenge implicit in true service meant that the king and his court were becoming increasingly remote from the people.

The next step in James's campaign was to obtain a parliament that would repeal the Test Acts. The same methods which had produced such a satisfactory result in 1685 were employed once more, although the criteria according to which men were sifted had changed. The disposition of office holders was now sampled by means of three standard questions: 1) if elected to Parliament, would they vote to repeal the penal laws and the Test Acts? 2) would they vote for candidates who had undertaken to do so? and 3) would they 'support the Declaration of Indulgence by living friendly with those of several persuasions as subjects of the same prince and as good Christians ought to do?'[25] The aggregated responses to these questions have divided modern historians. Some have argued that they should have alerted James to the depth of disquiet in the nation concerning the measures he was pursuing. Others have contended that, on the contrary, James was right to feel encouraged by the returns, which indicated that he had a good chance of obtaining a parliament that would be largely obedient to his wishes.

At any rate, James determined to press ahead with his plans. Accordingly he toughened his stance towards his former allies in the Church of England:

> In the country as a whole the place of the Tories was filled by dissenters and former Whigs, old enemies whom James now proposed to transform into the instruments of royal policy and strength. The Declaration of Indulgence, on 4 April 1687, represented the formal bid for their cooperation.[26]

On 27 April 1688 James reissued his Declaration of toleration and liberty of conscience, adding a postscript to the effect that he intended to summon a parliament by November. On 4 May he followed this up with an order in council to the clergy of the Church of England in which he instructed them to read – and thereby effectively to approve – the Declaration in their churches on two successive Sundays. The bishops were ordered to distribute the Declaration throughout their dioceses. It was an escalation that would rebound upon James in spectacular fashion.

On 6 April 1775 Samuel Johnson was dining with Boswell, Thomas Davies, John Moody the actor and 'Mr. Hicky, the painter' when the conversation turned critically to the later Stuarts. Johnson leaped to their defence:

> James the Second ... was a very good King, but unhappily believed that it was necessary for the salvation of his subjects that they should be Roman Catholicks. *He* had the merit of endeavouring to do what he thought was for the salvation of the souls of his subjects, till he lost a great Empire. *We*, who thought that we should *not* be saved if we were Roman Catholicks, had the merit of maintaining our religion, at the expence of submitting ourselves to the government of King William, (for it could not be done otherwise,) – to the government of one of the most worthless scoundrels that ever existed.[27]

For Johnson, James was a king tragically trapped by principle. Yet was it wise to attempt to change the national religion? Reason-of-state theorists earlier in the century, such as the duc de Rohan, had clearly seen the folly of it, arguing that the particular interest of the King of England is that '*He ought thoroughly to acquire the aduauncement of the Protestant Religion, euen with as much zeale as the King of Spaine appeares Protectour of the Catholike.*'[28]

THE SEVEN BISHOPS AND THE BIRTH OF A CATHOLIC HEIR

James's insistence that the Declaration of Indulgence be read out from the pulpit caused understandable agitation among the clergy of the Church of England. Some argued that merely to read out the Declaration did not imply approval, and that it should be complied with as a simple act of obedience. Others peered more searchingly into the likely consequences of doing as the king desired:

> the publishing this in such manner was only imposed on them to make them odious and contemptible to the whole Nation, for reading that which was intended for their ruin ... If they once yielded the point ... they were bound to read every declaration ... The King might make declarations in favour of all the points of Popery, and require them to read them: And they could not see where they must make their stops, if they did not now.[29]

These were the sentiments of the great majority of the clergy, and they found an echo on the bench. Sancroft, the Archbishop of Canterbury, after consultation, and in company with six bishops, drafted a petition to the king explaining why the clergy had decided not to obey his order. The arguments were overwhelmingly legal and political, rather than religious:

> this declaration being founded on such a dispensing power, as had been often declared illegal in Parliament, both in the year 1662 and in the year 1672, and in the beginning of his own reign, and was a matter of so great consequence to the whole Nation, both in Church and State; they could not in prudence, honour, and conscience, make themselves so far parties to it, as the publication of it once and again in God's house, and in the time of divine service, must amount to.[30]

The language of the petition was moderate and it had been presented respectfully. Nevertheless, James could see in it nothing but contumacy and disobedience. The bishops were cited to appear before the council. They were asked if they acknowledged the petition to be their own work. Having done so, they were charged with its publication. This they denied, saying that the source of any printed copies now in circulation must have originated from those close to the king. They were then required to appear in the Court of King's Bench, in the meantime being sent to the Tower.

The public response was extraordinary. The bishops were taken to the Tower by boat, and as they passed downstream the banks of the Thames were lined with people kneeling, asking their blessing and wishing them well. The eventual trial, in Westminster Hall, lasted longer than ten hours. The jury remained impanelled overnight, although it is said that they had reached their verdict very quickly, and had seemed to delay over it only out of prudence. When the verdict to acquit was announced on 29 June 1688, public rejoicing broke out: 'there were such shoutings, so long continued, and as it were echoed into the City, that all people were struck with it. Bonefires were made all about the streets. And the news going over the Nation, produced the like rejoycings and bonefires all *England* over.'[31]

The acquittal of the seven bishops was a terrible blow to James. He had sought a legal contest with the Church of England over whether the crown or the Church should prevail, but he had chosen his ground poorly, and the issue had been decided against him. At the same time, the depth and breadth of public disquiet concerning James's measures on questions of religion had been openly displayed in a manner that can only have encouraged resistance, and confirmed the growing disaffection of the majority.

James may have been angered by the turn events had taken, but he seems not to have been unnerved. The reason for his strange confidence is to be found in the fact that, against all prediction, Mary Beatrice had fallen pregnant in October 1687, and had given birth to a healthy boy on 10 June, nearly three weeks before the acquittal of the bishops. The birth was surrounded by suspicious circumstances. It had occurred a month before the due date, and the most trustworthy witnesses – including Princess Anne – had not been present:

> No cries were heard from the child: Nor was it shewed to those in the room. It was pretended, more air was necessary. The under dresser went out with the child, or somewhat else, in her arms to a dressing room, to which there was a door near the Queen's bed: But there was another entry to it from other apartments.[32]

Rumours soon began to circulate that the child was supposititious, and had been smuggled into St James's Palace in a warming pan. James indignantly rejected these slurs, and modern historians no longer take them seriously. Nevertheless, the scandalous story was influential in the increasingly tense later months of 1688.

The political implications of this birth were enormous. On 9 June, the heir presumptive was James's staunchly Protestant daughter Mary, the wife of William of Orange.

On the following day the heir apparent was the Catholic Prince James Francis Edward. The Protestant reversionary interest, which had both consoled Protestants alarmed by James's religious policy and acted as a restraint on James himself, was now destroyed: 'the birth of the Prince of Wales put an end to the "wait-for-better-times" strategy advocated by the likes of Halifax, since there was now little likelihood that James's policies would be reversed by his successor'.[33] A Roman Catholic Stuart dynasty now seemed to have been securely established.

The virtual simultaneity of the birth which James believed – wrongly, as it turned out – would cement his rule, and the verdict which pointed, on the contrary, to the evaporating public support which would play an important part in his downfall, was a vivid coincidence which seems, curiously, to have encouraged both James and his opponents. James could take comfort in the birth of a son. But those ranged against him had perhaps stronger reasons to feel emboldened: 'The government was quite powerless to halt the wave of rejoicing that spread out from London over the whole of England, sweeping most of the Dissenters with it. The birth of a Prince had given them the prospect of a Catholic dynasty in perpetuity: the trial of the seven bishops was a gratuitous demonstration of how a Catholic monarch treated Protestants who had always regarded him with the most devoted loyalty: their acquittal substituted contempt for fear. An incompetent despotism is a contradiction in terms.'[34]

The birth of the prince forced the hand of William of Orange. William was both James's nephew (being the son of James's sister, Mary) and his son-in-law (being the husband of James's daughter, also called Mary). He was himself therefore a Stuart, and moreover a Stuart whose ideas of monarchical authority were hardly less high than those of his uncle. William had been raised in the autocratic traditions of the Brabant aristocracy, and he was vigilant to defend the absolute character of his own rule. However they were later to be redescribed, and whatever was claimed on his behalf in his various manifestos, William's motives for involving himself in the affairs of England in 1688 had little to do with securing the liberties of Englishmen (in the early years of his reign he was very careful to keep the Whigs at a distance) and much more to do with securing his own dynastic interests, and those of his wife.

William had become head of state of the United Provinces in 1672. The belief which dominated all William's political thinking throughout his adult life was his conviction that Louis XIV aimed at establishing a universal monarchy, and that he must at all costs be prevented. This diagnosis of Louis's intentions was not shared by either Charles or James; indeed, it was not always and everywhere the view even of William's own subjects in the Netherlands, some of whom suspected that he exaggerated the threat from Louis in order to build up his own power. This difference of perspective on European politics between William and his uncles laid the ground for the history of tension, friction and misunderstanding between them.

In July 1681 William had travelled to England and had made comments suggesting support for Exclusion, to the annoyance of both Charles and James. Relations worsened when Monmouth sought refuge with William after the discovery of the Rye House Plot in 1683, and was cordially entertained by him. With the accession of James in 1685, matters deteriorated still further. Perhaps under the influence of Gilbert Burnet, who had gone into exile in the Netherlands and had become an adviser to William on English affairs, William began to believe more strongly that his English interests were being undermined by James. But James too had reasons to mistrust William. Confidence between the two men was impaired by the fact that both Argyll and Monmouth had planned their expeditions against James in, and launched them from, the Low Countries (although James later professed to be satisfied that William had not colluded in either attempt). For his part, William believed that James had not tried very hard to make Louis restore the Principality of Orange – territory in the south of France which was originally part of William's patrimony, but which had been occupied by French forces in 1680 and annexed to the French crown in 1685. When in 1686 James had sought William's approval for the repeal of the Test Acts, William had withheld it. While he was in favour of freedom of worship for both Dissenters and Catholics, he had explained, he nevertheless did not wish to destroy the special constitutional position of the Church of England, which he saw as depending on the Test Acts. James had been baffled and annoyed by William's response to his overtures.

James was to be even more annoyed in the early months of 1688, when William allowed his religious position to be laid out in a pamphlet, *Pensionary Fagel's Letter*, in which it was made clear that William would permit freedom of worship to both Dissenters and Catholics. This was a dramatic intervention in English politics. It threatened to render irrelevant James's tactical courting of the Dissenters, who now saw that William would give them all that they really wanted in the way of practical toleration, but would not demand of them the price that James asked for the same benefit, namely repeal of the Test Acts. At the same time, the pamphlet implicitly presented William as someone to whom Englishmen, anxious for their liberties, might turn for comfort and relief.

INVASION, REVOLUTION AND FLIGHT

It was against this backdrop of deteriorating relations between uncle and nephew that the dramatic events of 1688 were played out. Admiral Russell – cousin of the Lord William Russell executed in 1683 – had travelled to the Hague in May 1688, ostensibly to visit his sister, in fact to press William to intervene militarily in English affairs. William responded that 'if he was invited by some men of the best interest, and the most valued in the Nation, who should both in their own name, and in the name of others who trusted them, invite him to come and rescue the Nation and the Religion, he believed he could be ready by the end of *September*'.[35] Time, as all the actors in this drama appreciated, was tight:

> In the summer of 1688 many well-informed observers called
> for immediate action against James II. Their point was not

that James's regime was about to crumble but rather that if his opponents did not act with alacrity, James's position would be impregnable.[36]

The responsibility for procuring the signatories to the famous letter of invitation which was sent to William later that year fell to Henry Sidney, the brother of Algernon Sidney, the Whig martyr executed after the discovery of the Rye House Plot. Despite the numbers who knew of these treasonable preparations – 'many thousands', according to Burnet – secrecy was maintained.[37] Nevertheless, the motives of those who invited William to invade and the motives of William himself were not perfectly aligned:

> For those who invited him, William's purpose was to rescue our 'almost lost' liberties and religion; in reality William came so as to involve Britain in the war against France, and it can be argued that all the really revolutionary consequences of 1688 were the result of this involvement in a general European war rather than of the political settlement itself.[38]

As always, William's primary concern was with the continental struggle to frustrate the ambitions of Louis XIV. For him, the Englishman's religion and his liberties were in the end only useful pretexts for an invasion undertaken to ensure that the wealth and strength of England would, for the foreseeable future, be deployed against France.

Rumours concerning William's preparations began to spread during the summer of 1688, although he did his best to mislead by seeming to have intentions towards the east and an intervention in German affairs. James was very poorly supplied with information from the Hague, but the French had a much more professional system for gathering intelligence, and the fruits of this were passed on to James. Yet James discounted it: 'whatever the designs of the *Dutch* might be, he was sure they were not against him'.[39]

What can explain this passiveness on James's part? On the one hand, James was sure that members of his own family would not rise against him. On the other, there was the question of timing. In the late seventeenth century warfare was still very much a seasonal activity. With every month that passed, the window for military action grew smaller:

> James has been accused of making too few martial preparations too late, a tardiness that cost him his three thrones. Most of this adverse criticism is unreasonable. He was indeed slow to appreciate the danger from the Netherlands but, as a man with considerable military and naval experience of conventional warfare, he simply did not believe that William would be physically or strategically able to launch an offensive operation within the campaigning season of 1688.[40]

Furthermore, James was also certain that the States General would not allow William to go adventuring with much of the armed strength of the United Provinces when Louis XIV was manoeuvring in ways that seemed to threaten them. But when French forces were in fact unleashed they were sent against an objective far to the south-east – against the Rhine fortress of Philippsburg – and in consequence the

French threat to the Netherlands was suspended. A Dutch invasion of England late in the year was still a very risky proposition, but the danger of leaving the way clear for a French invasion had, for the time being, been removed. When the French went into action on the Rhine, William realized that he need no longer fear immediate French reprisals were he to invade England.

Accordingly in October 1688 William marched his troops from Nijmegen to the North Sea coast, where they were embarked: 'Never was so great a design executed in so short a time. A transport fleet of five hundred vessels was hired in three days time. All things, as soon as they were ordered, were got to be so quickly ready, that we were amazed at the dispatch.'[41] William's army comprised some 14,000 men. At the same time copies of his Declaration were circulated, in which he set out his reasons for intervening in England. The mistakes Monmouth had made in his manifesto three years earlier were carefully avoided. William placed the emphasis on the need for a free parliament to settle the questions which confronted the nation. The unwisdom of James's policies was touched on, but Monmouth's furious rhetoric of crimes, poison and tyranny was sensibly left to one side.

The Dutch fleet first set sail on 19 October but was driven back by storms and adverse winds from the west, which lasted nearly two weeks. However, on 1 November the wind shifted to the east – the famous 'Protestant wind' – and the fleet moved out again. The easterly wind had a double advantage: it allowed the Dutch to sail down the Channel, and it kept the English fleet, which James had strengthened in the spring of 1688, harmlessly pinned down in the mouth of the Thames. Four days later, on 5 November – a day auspicious in the Protestant calendar as the anniversary of the discovery of the Gunpowder Plot – 'a soft and happy gale of wind carried in the whole Fleet in four hours time into Torbay'.[42]

By mid September even James had had to accept the unwelcome truth that his nephew intended to invade England; what he had still regarded as only an outside possibility even a month before, he now realized was an overwhelming probability. Belatedly he began to raise additional troops. By the end of October the nominal strength of James's army had been increased to some 40,000 men. But that figure included non-combatants (such as officers' servants) and large numbers of low-grade, probably useless, new levies. There were also problems of equipment and supply. Nevertheless, the effective fighting strength of James's army was approximately double that of William's. At the heart of both armies were some crack professional regiments and an experienced officer corps.[43]

James's hurried military preparations were accompanied by hectic political back-pedalling. He announced his intention to call a parliament in November, a move which the French ambassador Barrillon read shrewdly as a tactic dictated by the current emergency, and not expressive of any deep change of heart or mind: 'this proclamation of a Parliament will please the nation and render odious any enterprise which the Prince of Orange might undertake'.[44] James also met the bishops, led by Archbishop Sancroft. He explained that 'he had never intended to carry things further than to an equal liberty of conscience: He desired, they would declare their abhorrence of this invasion, and that they would offer him their advice, what was fit for him to do'.[45] Their advice amounted to a comprehensive retreat: the removal of Catholics from office, the upholding of the Test Acts, the restoration of borough charters, the reinstating of the fellows of Magdalen, the suppression of the Ecclesiastical Commission, and a free (i.e. un-gerrymandered) parliament – nothing less, then, than a complete undoing of everything James had sought to bring about on the domestic front for the past three years. James gave in on all points, except the summoning of Parliament. When William's fleet was driven back and detained in harbour by westerly storms James's confidence surged for a while, and he recalled the order for the reinstatement of the fellows of Magdalen: a move 'which plainly shewed,' as Burnet tartly remarks, 'what it was that drove the Court into so much compliance, and how long it was like to last'.[46]

Once William had landed, however, it was clear that the future of the nation would be resolved by arms, and not by political bargaining. James could have waited for William to advance from the West Country and have offered battle nearer London. But clearly to do so would have given the invading forces a chance to get over the effects of their sea voyage and also to be strengthened by possible desertions. James therefore decided to advance to meet William, leaving London on 17 November and arriving at Salisbury two days later. At this point the king was struck down, banally enough, by severe nosebleeds:

The King wanted support: For his spirits sunk extreamly. His blood was in such fermentation, that he was bleeding much at the nose, which returned oft upon him every day. He sent many spies over to us. They all took his money, and came and joined themselves to the Prince, none of them returning to him. So that he had no intelligence brought him of what the Prince was doing, but what common reports brought him, which magnified our numbers, and made him think we were coming near him, while we were still at *Exeter*.[47]

While James was confined to his bed, units of his army began to defect to William. Sick, unnerved and misinformed, James decided to retreat towards London. This did nothing to reduce the rate of desertion, which if anything increased in volume and significance. James's morale was hit hard when those close to him, such as John Churchill, the future Duke of Marlborough, and the Duke of Grafton, an illegitimate child of his brother Charles, went over to the invaders. When he arrived back in London, he was greeted by the news that his daughter Anne had also thrown in her lot with William. On 3 December the commander of James's army, the Earl of Feversham, informed him that the loyalty of the army was no longer to be relied on. Public order was breaking down. The city had been raised to a frenzy by a further Declaration, purporting to enjoy William's approval but in fact the handiwork of radicals in his entourage, warning that Catholics, and particularly Irish units from James's army, were planning bloody revenge. William was continuing to advance on London, and enjoyed either the active support, or the passive acquiescence, of the population of the counties through which he passed. There were no engagements between the two forces, aside from minor skirmishes at Winkington in Dorset and at Reading.

James held a meeting with those peers who were in London, and sought their advice. They recommended opening negotiations with William, and reluctantly James agreed. James's envoys met William at Hungerford. One of them was Halifax, who had a private meeting with Burnet, then in William's entourage:

> he took occasion to ask me ... if we had a mind to have the King in our hands. I said, by no means; for we would not hurt his person. He asked next, what if he had a mind to go away. I said, nothing was so much to be wished for. This I told the Prince. And he approved of both my answers.[48]

Burnet is never guilty of underestimating the importance of the role he played in public affairs. Even so, this stolen moment of quiet conversation is a fascinating fragment of secret history. William's formal responses to James's overtures were, on the face of it, moderate:

> He desired a Parliament might be presently called, that no men should continue in any employment, who were not qualified by law, and had not taken the Tests, that the Tower of *London* might be put in the keeping of the City; that the Fleet, and all the strong places of the Kingdom, might be put in the hands of Protestants; that a proportion of the revenue might be set off for the pay of the Prince's Army; and that

during the sitting of the Parliament, the Armies of both sides might not come within twenty miles of *London*; but, that the Prince might come on to *London*, and have the same number of his guards about him, that the King kept about his person.[49]

James reportedly said that he had not expected such good terms. However, he placed his trust less in William's public engagements than in the private indications of what he desired and would accept.

Under the strain of these repeated blows, James's nerve eventually broke. On 9 December he sent the queen and the Prince of Wales to France. On the evening of the next day, he surreptitiously followed them. In a petulant gesture, so expressive of his lack of understanding of political realities, James threw the Great Seal into the river as he fled, hoping thereby to immobilize public business. Burnet pauses in his narrative at this point:

> Thus a great King, who had a good Army and a strong Fleet, did choose rather to abandon all, than either to expose himself to any danger with that part of the Army that was still firm to him, or to stay and see the issue of a Parliament ... It was not possible to put a good construction on any part of the dishonourable scene which he then acted.[50]

It is a judgement in which even those prone to spasms of Jacobite sentiment would agree. Swift would include James's conduct at this crisis of his fortunes in the list he compiled of mean and contemptible figures in history.[51]

Even now James's indignities were not at an end. He was intercepted by some Kentish fishermen, and, after some rough handling, returned to London, where he was 'welcomed with expressions of joy by great numbers: So slight and unstable a thing is a multitude, and so soon altered.'[52] But even James, prone as he was to irrational confidence, could not deceive himself that his reign could be prolonged. Effective power had passed from him. As William entered London, James withdrew to Rochester, having refused to go to Ham House, presumably because it was less well placed from the point of view of escape, ostensibly because it was not large enough to house his retinue. He arrived in Rochester on 19 December, where he remained for a few days watching for an opportunity to get away. It arrived on 24 December. Early the following morning, James landed on French soil at Ambleteuse. Although in the letter he left behind on the table in his lodgings he asserted that 'he was going to seek for foreign aid to restore him to his Throne', James never again set foot in England.[53] It was an extraordinary reversal:

The more we reflect on the fall of James II, the more remarkable it seems. James was both powerful and popular when he came to the throne in 1685. The challenge of the Whigs had been contained and radicalism seemed to be a spent force, as testified by the speed and ease with which the rebellions of Argyll and Monmouth were put down. The vast majority of James's subjects, including those who held power, believed that their king ruled by divine right and was absolute. Yet James ended up being resisted by people who believed in non-resistance, and was held to have done wrong by people who believed that the king could do no wrong.[54]

4
Exile and Death

THE NEW POLITICAL SETTLEMENT IN ENGLAND AND THE IRISH CAMPAIGN

On his arrival in France James was greeted by Louis as an injured brother sovereign. He was given the use of the palace of St Germain-en-Laye, and provided with a generous pension. On the other side of the Channel William had assumed control of the government in the absence of any alternative, but the form of the post-Jacobite settlement had yet to be decided. A convention was summoned (it could not be called a parliament, since a monarch is essential to a parliament: and, depending on your point of view, either the throne was vacant or the reigning sovereign was unable to be present).

There were three possible ways forward. Some thought that James should be called back to the throne, but required to give securities in respect of law and religion which would satisfy his subjects' still vivid anxieties concerning popery, arbitrary government and the use James had made of his dispensing power. Others recognized that the right to the crown remained in James, but that his record of maladministration meant that a regency, to be exercised by William, should be set up. A third group, less afraid of strong measures, advocated setting James aside and offering the crown to William.

Apparently the simplest, this third option in fact entailed immense legal and religious complexities. How could an anointed king be set aside? Even some of those who had been prepared to oppose James's actions in Church and State, such as Archbishop Sancroft, could see no way past the obligations created by the oath they had taken to James on his accession. Some three hundred clergy – the so-called Non-Jurors – followed Sancroft in a principled refusal to swear the oaths of allegiance required by the new regime.

The two cardinal points of discussion in the Convention were over the existence and nature of an original contract, if there were such a thing; and over whether or not James could be said to have abdicated, when there were such clear signs of force having been used against him. The debates were long and detailed, and had a rich afterlife in the politics of the ensuing decades. The Convention eventually decided that James had broken the original contract and had abdicated the throne, creating a vacancy which it fell to them to fill. Accordingly, they resolved on 28 January that:

> king James the second, having endeavoured to subvert the constitution of the kingdom, by breaking the original contract, between king and people, and by the advice of Jesuits and other wicked persons having violated the fundamental laws, and having withdrawn himself out of this kingdom, has abdicated the government; and that the throne is thereby vacant.[1]

On 13 February 1689 the crown was offered jointly to William and Mary. In addition the Convention passed a Bill of Rights, in which the chief heads of James's maladministration were specified, and the customary liberties of the people of England were laid down. The Bill of Rights also altered the succession, specifying that any future English monarch could not be a member of the Roman Catholic Church:

> And whereas it hath beene found by Experience that it is inconsistent with the Safety and Welfare of this Protestant Kingdome to be governed by a Popish Prince or by any King or Queene marrying a Papist the said Lords Spirituall and Temporall and Commons doe further pray that it may be enacted That all and every person and persons that is are or shall be reconciled to or shall hold Communion with the See or Church of Rome or shall professe the Popish Religion or shall marry a Papist shall be excluded and be for ever uncapeable to inherit possesse or enjoy the Crowne and Government of this Realme and Ireland and the Dominions thereunto belonging or any part of the same or to have use or exercise any Regall Power Authoritie or Jurisdiction within the same . . .[2]

This momentous change, so expressive of what James's subjects had found most deeply offensive in his behaviour, was not the subject of a separate clause in the bill. It was placed inconspicuously in a large block of text at the end concerning the terms on which William and Mary jointly accepted the crown. The Bill of Rights was intended to be a 'new *Magna Charta*'.[3] In fact it did much more than merely declare and republish existing rights and laws. It created a new political landscape which would endure until the Great Reform Bill of 1832.

By his flight to France James had surrendered control of England, but he still nominally ruled two realms, Scotland and Ireland. The Scots very quickly fell into line with the disposition of affairs in England. The whole kingdom, with the temporary exception of Edinburgh Castle (which was held by the Catholic Duke of Gordon), declared for William. When William assumed control of the government of England, the Duke of Hamilton co-ordinated an address to William closely modelled on the English address, and the government of the whole island of Britain thus fell into William's hands.

Ireland, however, remained under the control of Tyrconnell, who immediately set about raising additional forces, and who invited James to join him there and to use Ireland as the base from which to recover Scotland and England. Louis's intelligence suggested that Tyrconnell's plan was feasible, given French support. James landed in Kinsale in March 1689 and made his way towards Dublin. From there he moved further north with a large army assembled by Tyrconnell to attack the Protestant rebels in Ulster. It was a campaign bedevilled by practical problems of supply and poor military discipline, and undermined by divided aims among its leaders. James's intention was to use Ireland as a springboard from which to attack England. Tyrconnell's ambitions were focused much more exclusively on Ireland, where he wished to restore the political and economic ascendancy of the Catholic majority, and to install James as a Catholic monarch – a move which would have made it impossible for James to exploit the English disenchantment with William which had set in very quickly after his and Mary's coronation. James's army became bogged down in the siege of Derry, which held out until they were relieved at the end of July 1689. In August William's general, Schomberg, arrived with a large army. He was followed in June 1690 by William himself, with yet more troops. On 30 June the two armies encountered one another on the River Boyne, just north of Dublin. James was outmanoeuvred by William and fled, first to Dublin, thereafter to Duncannon, whence he embarked for France on 3 July.

FINAL YEARS

The final decade or so of James's life at St Germain was filled with political apathy and superstitious devotion. Although various Jacobite plots for his restoration were set in motion during the 1690s, James accepted their failure with equanimity. He now tended to see the reversals of his later years as God's punishment for the sinfulness of his youth. He made annual visits to the monastery of La Trappe, on each occasion staying there several days and passing the time 'in long Meditations and spiritual Conferences with the Abbot and his Confessor'.[4] In 1697, as part of the Treaty of Ryswick, Louis was obliged to recognize William as King of England, and to agree to take no further practical steps towards James's restoration. Nothing now seemed able to improve James's political prospects. In March 1701 his health began visibly to fail: he suffered a stroke and internal bleeding. The end came on 5 September, after several days of steady decline.

In his will James had asked to be buried in Westminster Abbey, but this was clearly impossible. Instead, his funeral followed the customs of the French monarchy. His body was embalmed, and the heart, brain and entrails removed for separate burial. The eviscerated corpse was placed in the English Benedictine College in Paris. It was kept above ground in a bier, ready to be returned to Westminster Abbey whenever the Stuart dynasty should be restored. His heart was sent to the Visitandine convent in Paris, where it lay alongside the heart of his mother. His entrails were buried in the church of St Germain-en-Laye. All these buildings were destroyed during the French Revolution. His brain was deposited in the chapel of the Scots College in Paris, in the rue du Cardinal Lemoine, where a marble monument to the last Roman Catholic King of England yet survives.[5]

Notes

1. THE VARIETIES OF WHIG HISTORY

1. W. A. Speck, *Reluctant Revolutionaries: Englishmen and the Revolution of 1688* (Oxford: Oxford University Press, 1988), p. 246: hereafter Speck, *Reluctant Revolutionaries*. For a contrasting view of 1688 as little more than a 'palace coup', see J. C. D. Clark, *English Society 1660–1832: Religion, Ideology and Politics during the Ancien Regime* (Cambridge: Cambridge University Press, 2000).
2. Steve Pincus, *1688: The First Modern Revolution* (New Haven and London: Yale University Press, 2009), pp. 6 and 8: hereafter Pincus, *1688*.
3. Herbert Butterfield, *The Whig Interpretation of History* (London: G. Bell and Sons, 1931).
4. For example and most recently, J. R. Jones, W. A. Speck, J. C. D. Clark, Tim Harris and Steve Pincus.
5. Thomas Babington Macaulay, *The History of England from the Accession of James the Second*, 11th edn, 4 vols (London, 1856), vol. 3, pp. 648–9: hereafter Macaulay, *History of England*.
6. Macaulay, *History of England*, vol. 4, pp. 386–7.
7. Pincus, *1688*, pp. 5–6.
8. J. P. Kenyon, *Revolution Principles: The Politics of Party 1689–1720* (Cambridge: Cambridge University Press, 1977), pp. 42–3: hereafter Kenyon, *Revolution Principles*.
9. Anon., *Quadriennium Jacobi, or the History of the Reign of King James II* (London, 1689), 'Preface': hereafter *Quadriennium*.
10. *Quadriennium*, 'Preface'.

2. DUKE OF YORK

1. John Miller, *James II* (New Haven and London: Yale University Press, 2000), p. 2: hereafter Miller, *James II*.
2. Edward Hyde, Earl of Clarendon, *The History of the Rebellion and Civil Wars in England*, ed. W. Dunn Macray, 6 vols (Oxford: Clarendon Press, 1888), vol. 2, pp. 361–2, book VI, § 85: hereafter Clarendon, *History*.
3. Miller, *James II*, p. 3.
4. *Bishop Burnet's History of His Own Time*, 2 vols (London, 1724 and 1734), vol. 1, p. 169: hereafter Burnet, *History*.

5. Clarendon, *History*, vol. 4, pp. 251–3; book X, § 116–18.

6. Clarendon, *History*, vol. 4, p. 251; book X, § 116.

7. Clarendon, *History*, vol. 4, p. 327; book XI, § 20.

8. Burnet, *History*, vol. 1, pp. 720–21.

9. Burnet, *History*, vol. 1, p. 618.

10. Clarendon, *History*, vol. 5, pp. 224–5; book XIII, § 122. Cf. also *The Diary of Samuel Pepys*, ed. Robert Latham and William Matthews, 11 vols (London: G. Bell and Sons, 1970–83), vol. 8, p. 431, n. 1: hereafter Pepys, *Diary*.

11. Burnet, *History*, vol. 1, p. 613.

12. Pepys, *Diary*, vol. 8, p. 431 and n. 1.

13. Burnet, *History*, vol. 1, pp. 170–71 and 613.

14. Quoted in Miller, *James II*, p. 12.

15. Burnet, *History*, vol. 1, p. 169.

16. Charles James Fox, *A History of the Early Part of the Reign of James the Second; with an Introductory Chapter* (London, 1808), p. 16: hereafter Fox, *James II*.

17. *The Diary of John Evelyn*, sel. and ed. John Bowle, 'The World's Classics' (Oxford and New York: Oxford University Press, 1985), p. 360: hereafter Evelyn, *Diary*.

18. 'Conciliation with the Colonies', in Edmund Burke, *A Philosophical Enquiry into the Sublime and Beautiful and Other Pre-Revolutionary Writings*, ed. David Womersley (London: Penguin Books, 1998), p. 355: hereafter Burke, *Enquiry*.

19. 'American Taxation', in Burke, *Enquiry*, p. 329.

20. [Chevalier Ramsay], *The History of Henri de la Tour d'Auvergne, Viscount de Turenne*, 2 vols (London, 1735), vol. 2, p. 476: hereafter *Turenne*. Cf. Clarendon, *History*, vol. 5, p. 247; book XIII, § 148.

21. Francis Brettonneau, *An Abridgment of the Life of James II* (London, 1704), p. 7: hereafter Brettonneau, *Life*.

22. They were published as an appendix in *Turenne*.

23. *Turenne*, vol. 2, p. 511.

24. Burnet, *History*, vol. 1, p. 619.

25. Evelyn, *Diary*, p. 182.

26. David Hume, *The History of England*, ed. W. B. Todd, 6 vols (Indianapolis: Liberty Fund, 1983), vol. 6, p. 139: hereafter Hume, *History*.

27. Pepys, *Diary*, vol. 9, p. 132 and n. 1.

28. Pepys, *Diary*, vol. 9, p. 290 and n. 1.

29. Quoted in Miller, *James II*, p. 42.

30. Burnet, *History*, vol. 1, p. 170.

31. Ibid.

32. Evelyn, *Diary*, p. 185.

33. Burnet, *History*, vol. 1, p. 228.

34. Pepys, *Diary*, vol. 7, pp. 323 and 320.

35. Burnet, *History*, vol. 1, p. 169.

36. Pepys, *Diary*, vol. 5, p. 21; cf. also vol. 4, p. 367 and vol. 5, pp. 167 and 185–6.

37. Burnet, *History*, vol. 1, p. 170.

38. Pepys, *Diary*, vol. 6, p. 122. For another occasion when James was 'under sail', see Evelyn, *Diary*, p. 246.

39. *Second Advice to a Painter*, ll. 187–8.

40. See Pincus, *1688*, pp. 90, 375, 381 and 383.

41. Evelyn, *Diary*, p. 212.

42. Burnet, *History*, vol. 1, p. 168. This 'constant journal' was presumably the basis of the archive of James's personal papers that were smuggled into France in the

aftermath of 1688, held in the Scots College in Paris, but subsequently destroyed during the French Revolution.

43. Pepys, *Diary*, vol. 8, pp. 304 and 264–5.
44. Pepys, *Diary*, vol. 8, p. 269.
45. Burnet, *History*, vol. 1, p. 613.
46. Pepys, *Diary*, vol. 8, pp. 410 (early willingness to sacrifice Clarendon) and 406 (support for Clarendon).
47. Pepys, *Diary*, vol. 8, p. 434.
48. Pepys, *Diary*, vol. 8, p. 431.
49. John Miller, 'Anne Hyde', *ODNB*.
50. Brettonneau, *Life*, p. 13 and Miller, *James II*, p. 59; note however the reservations of Speck on the point of timing in *ODNB*.
51. 'The Duke was now [the period leading up to the Declaration of Indulgence in 1672] known to be a Papist: And the Duchess was much suspected' (Burnet, *History*, vol. 1, p. 308).
52. Burnet, *History*, vol. 1, p. 458.
53. Brettonneau, *Life*, pp. 7–9.
54. Burnet, *History*, vol. 1, pp. 720–21.
55. Anon., *The Secret History of the Reigns of K. Charles II. and K. James II.* (London, 1690), p. 154: hereafter *Secret History*.
56. 'The Duke ... said, he would be ready always to comply with the King's pleasure in every thing' (Burnet, *History*, vol. 1, p. 409): said in 1677, concerning the marriage of his daughter Mary to William of Orange.
57. Burnet, *History*, vol. 1, p. 169. See also, however, the account of his conversion James wrote in the letter he sent to his daughter Mary in an attempt to convert her (Burnet, *History*, vol. 1, pp. 720–22).
58. Burnet, *History*, vol. 1, pp. 170 and 590; cf. also p. 309.
59. Pepys, *Diary*, vol. 9, pp. 163–4.
60. Burnet, *History*, vol. 1, p. 309.
61. Brettonneau, *Life*, p. 11.
62. Burnet, *History*, vol. 1, p. 310.
63. John 18:38.
64. Miller, *James II*, pp. 59–62.
65. Burnet, *History*, vol. 1, p. 603.
66. Burnet, *History*, vol. 1, p. 308.
67. Brettonneau, *Life*, p. 11.
68. Burnet, *History*, vol. 1, p. 347.
69. Brettonneau, *Life*, p. 14 (italic reversed). Cf. Romans 3:7–9.
70. Burnet, *History*, vol. 1, p. 345.
71. Burnet, *History*, vol. 1, p. 352.
72. Burnet, *History*, vol. 1, p. 438.
73. Hume, *History*, vol. 6, p. 251.
74. Burnet, *History*, vol. 1, p. 438.
75. Burnet, *History*, vol. 1, p. 452.
76. Burnet, *History*, vol. 1, p. 455.
77. Miller, *James II*, p. 98.
78. Burnet, *History*, vol. 1, p. 344.
79. *The Prose Works of Andrew Marvell*, ed. Annabel Patterson, Martin Dzelzainis, Nicholas von Maltzahn and N. H. Keeble, 2 vols (New Haven and London: Yale University Press, 2003), vol. 2, p. 225.

80. Burnet, *History*, vol. 1, p. 345.
81. *Memoirs of the English Affairs, Chiefly Naval ... Written by His Royal Highness James Duke of York* (London, 1729), p. xvi.
82. Fox, *James II*, p. 72.
83. Fox, *James II*, p. 165.
84. Burnet, *History*, vol. 1, p. 409.
85. On the Popish Plot, see still J. P. Kenyon, *The Popish Plot* (London: Heinemann, 1972).
86. Burnet, *History*, vol. 1, p. 424.
87. Burnet, *History*, vol. 1, p. 424.
88. Burnet, *History*, vol. 1, p. 424.
89. J. R. Jones, *The First Whigs: The Politics of the Exclusion Crisis 1678–1683* (London: Oxford University Press, 1961), p. 21: hereafter Jones, *First Whigs*.
90. Burnet, *History*, vol. 1, p. 437.
91. Miller, *James II*, p. 2.
92. Burnet, *History*, vol. 1, p. 427.
93. Burnet, *History*, vol. 1, p. 429.
94. Burnet, *History*, vol. 1, p. 451.
95. Fox, *James II*, p. 36.
96. Burnet, *History*, vol. 1, p. 452.
97. On which see Jones, *First Whigs*.
98. Burnet, *History*, vol. 1, p. 455.
99. Miller, *James II*, p. 95.
100. John Dryden, *Absalom and Achitophel*, ll. 152–62.
101. Quoted in Tim Harris, *ODNB*.
102. *A Letter from a Person of Quality to his Friend in the Country* (1675), p. 1.
103. Burnet, *History*, vol. 1, p. 457.
104. Burnet, *History*, vol. 1, p. 458.
105. Burnet, *History*, vol. 1, p. 530.
106. Burnet, *History*, vol. 1, p. 467.
107. Jones, *First Whigs*, p. 2.
108. Miller, *James II*, p. 111.
109. Burnet, *History*, vol. 1, pp. 487–8.
110. J. R. Jones, *The Revolution of 1688 in England* (London: Weidenfeld and Nicolson, 1972), p. 43: hereafter Jones, *1688*.
111. Burnet, *History*, vol. 1, p. 474.
112. Burnet, *History*, vol. 1, p. 583; cf. Ayloffe's retort to James when being questioned (op. cit., p. 634).
113. Macaulay, *History*, vol. 1, p. 498.
114. Burnet, *History*, vol. 1, pp. 510–11.
115. Burnet, *History*, vol. 1, p. 514.
116. Burnet, *History*, vol. 1, p. 524.
117. Burnet, *History*, vol. 1, p. 527.
118. Burnet, *History*, vol. 1, pp. 619 and 582–3.
119. So named because of the Latin phrase used in the royal writ obliging the recipient to show 'by what warrant' or authority a particular office or franchise is held or claimed (*OED*).
120. Burnet, *History*, vol. 1, p. 527.
121. Burnet, *History*, vol. 1, p. 568.
122. Burnet, *History*, vol. 1, p. 625.

123. Burnet, *History*, vol. 1, p. 543; cf. pp. 633–4.
124. Burnet, *History*, vol. 1, p. 606.
125. Burnet, *History*, vol. 1, p. 610.
126. Burnet, *History*, vol. 1, p. 607.
127. See, e.g., *Secret History*, p. 183: but cf. Burnet, *History*, vol. 1, p. 610. The accusation that James poisoned his brother would, notoriously, form part of the manifesto distributed by Monmouth during his invasion later in the year (Burnet, *History*, vol. 1, p. 641).
128. *The Memoirs of the Honorable Sir John Reresby, Baronet* (London, 1734), p. 108.

3. KING OF ENGLAND, SCOTLAND AND IRELAND

1. Quoted in Miller, *James II*, p. 120.
2. Burnet, *History*, vol. 1, p. 620.
3. Burnet, *History*, vol. 1, p. 637.
4. On whom see J. P. Kenyon, *Robert Spencer, Earl of Sunderland 1641–1702* (London, New York and Toronto: Longmans, Green and Co., 1958): hereafter Kenyon, *Sunderland*.
5. Kenyon, *Sunderland*, p. 84.
6. *Memoirs of the Marshal Duke of Berwick. Written by Himself*, 2 vols (London, 1779), vol. 1, p. 32.
7. Burnet, *History*, vol. 1, p. 626.
8. Ibid.
9. Quoted in Miller, *James II*, p. 136.
10. Burnet, *History*, vol. 1, p. 664.
11. Burnet, *History*, vol. 1, p. 671.
12. Burnet, *History*, vol. 1, p. 667.
13. Burnet, *History*, vol. 1, p. 672.
14. Burnet, *History*, vol. 1, p. 711.
15. Quoted in Miller, *James II*, pp. 175–6.
16. Speck, *Reluctant Revolutionaries*, p. 171.
17. On which, see most recently and most fully Pincus, *1688*.
18. Burnet, *History*, vol. 1, p. 675.
19. Ibid.
20. Burnet, *History*, vol. 1, pp. 669–70.
21. Burnet, *History*, vol. 1, p. 699.
22. Burnet, *History*, vol. 1, p. 700.
23. Burnet, *History*, vol. 1, p. 701.
24. Burnet, *History*, vol. 1, p. 720.
25. Burnet, *History*, vol. 1, p. 719.
26. Jones, *1688*, p. 99.
27. James Boswell, *The Life of Samuel Johnson*, ed. David Womersley (London: Penguin Books, 2008), pp. 444–5.
28. Duc de Rohan, *A Treatise of the Interest of the Princes and States of Christendome* ('Paris', 1640), p. 37.

29. Burnet, *History*, vol. 1, p. 737.
30. Burnet, *History*, vol. 1, p. 739.
31. Burnet, *History*, vol. 1, p. 744.
32. Burnet, *History*, vol. 1, p. 752.
33. Tim Harris, *Revolution: The Great Crisis of the British Monarchy, 1685–1720* (London: Allen Lane, 2006), p. 271: hereafter Harris, *Revolution*.
34. Kenyon, *Sunderland*, p. 200.
35. Burnet, *History*, vol. 1, p. 746.
36. Pincus, *1688*, p. 212.
37. Burnet, *History*, vol. 1, p. 766.
38. Jones, *1688*, p. 190.
39. Burnet, *History*, vol. 1, p. 766.
40. John Childs, *The Army, James II, and the Glorious Revolution* (Manchester: Manchester University Press, 1980), p. 177: hereafter Childs, *Army*.
41. Burnet, *History*, vol. 1, p. 781.
42. Burnet, *History*, vol. 1, p. 788.
43. For the military dimension of 1688, see Childs, *Army*.
44. Quoted in Miller, *James II*, p. 196.
45. Burnet, *History*, vol. 1, p. 784.
46. Burnet, *History*, vol. 1, pp. 784–5.
47. Burnet, *History*, vol. 1, p. 791.
48. Burnet, *History*, vol. 1, pp. 794–5.
49. Burnet, *History*, vol. 1, p. 795.
50. Burnet, *History*, vol. 1, p. 796.
51. *The Prose Writings of Jonathan Swift*, ed. Herbert Davis et al., 16 vols (Oxford: Basil Blackwell, 1939–74), vol. 5, p. 85.
52. Burnet, *History*, vol. 1, p. 799.
53. Burnet, *History*, vol. 1, p. 804.
54. Harris, *Revolution*, p. 478.

4. EXILE AND DEATH

1. Quoted in Speck, *Reluctant Revolutionaries*, p. 96.
2. http://www.legislation.gov.uk/aep/WillandMarSess2/1/2.
3. Burnet, *History*, vol. 1, p. 822.
4. Bretonneau, *Life*, p. 71.
5. See *Country Life*, 25 June 2014, pp. 114–17.

Bibliographical Essay

When James fled to France in 1688, he had sent after him a substantial volume of papers. According to Charles Fox, who saw them, they comprised ten manuscript volumes of memoirs, and four volumes of correspondence.[1] On James's death these papers were deposited in the Scots College in Paris, but were destroyed during the French Revolution. They are thought, however, to have informed, in ways that are now hard to pin down, Dicconson's *Life of James II*, edited by J. S. Clarke and published in 1816, and the earlier work of James Macpherson.[2]

Contemporary accounts of James include the writings of two celebrated diarists. Pepys gives us an incomparably intimate portrait of the Duke of York in the late 1660s.[3] Evelyn supplies some colourful touches, and the greater breadth of his diary, extending as it does as far as 1706, bestows on it a particular authority.[4] Clarendon's *History of the Rebellion* is valuable for what it tells us of the dealings between Charles I and his young children.[5] The *Memoirs* of Sir John Reresby give us an account of James's reign delivered from the position of a well-placed insider.[6]

The histories of James's reign written in the immediate aftermath of his flight are sometimes vigorous pieces of work, but they are too often vitiated by partisanship to repay the general reader. Burnet's *History of His Own Time*, however, falls into a different category.[7] Burnet was attacked bitterly during his lifetime, and modern historians have been quick to scorn his work. His history was indeed written from a certain standpoint, and in order to justify the cause that had prevailed. But its vulgar Whiggism is easily separated from a fascinating core of detailed information, much of it obtained at first hand by one who was sometimes close to the centre of the events he describes. Hume gives us an elegant and philosophical narrative, not remarkable for any independent discoveries, but a useful corrective to Burnet; and no time is wasted which is spent reading even the least trifle which dropped from the pen of Hume.[8] Fox's *A History of the Early Part of the Reign of James the Second; with an Introductory Chapter* is incomplete, but it is marked by the author's sharp political intelligence, and it contains some wonderful, penetrating formulations: it displays to the full both Fox's laziness and his brilliance.[9] Macaulay has become the 'Aunt Sally' of modern historians of the later seventeenth century – he is the great predecessor on whom they must prove their own competence by destroying his. In some respects, Macaulay's *History* presents us with an intensified version of the problem posed by Burnet.[10] The scholarly underpinnings of his narrative are considerable, but the moralizing tendentiousness of his interpretation tends to obscure them. It is hard to see how Macaulay's *History* could have its authority restored, at least among historians. On the other hand, his work should always command the interest, and even the respect, of the general reader. It was, after all, the narrative of the reign of James II that was accepted as authoritative for nearly a century.

The recent debate on the reign of James is almost an epitome of the modes and fashions of modern academic historiography. The dislodgement of the 'Whig Interpretation of History' begun by Herbert Butterfield has been eagerly pursued by his successors, although few of them have been notable for any interest in mapping the actual variations within that Whig interpretation – indeed, few of them show any sign of having attentively read what they lightly dismiss. J. R. Jones was notable for being the first modern historian to consider James's policies on their own terms, and in a perspective free from an overpowering awareness of how events had actually turned out.[11] His defence of both the technical legality and the practical feasibility of James's policies dropped a depth charge into the waters of Stuart history whose explosive energies have even now perhaps not been fully measured. Bill Speck offered a partial rehabilitation of Macaulay, and his lead has been followed by Tim Harris.[12] Steve Pincus has written the most widely researched and controversial history of 1688: a book which manages, in virtuoso fashion, to throw down gauntlets in the direction of both the Whigs and the revisionists.[13] John Miller's careful and searching biography is the best full-length modern treatment of James's life, although it can now usefully be supplemented by Bill Speck's excellent article on James in the *ODNB*.[14] Finally, and most recently, Scott Sowerby has attempted to rescue James's policy of toleration from its contemporary and more recent detractors, who have tended to deride it as a transparently tactical move.[15]

1. Fox, *James II*, p. xix, n. *.
2. James Macpherson, *Original Papers; Containing the Secret History of Great Britain, from the Restoration, to the Accession of the House of Hannover*, 2 vols (London, 1775).
3. *The Diary of Samuel Pepys*, ed. Robert Latham and William Matthews, 11 vols (London: G. Bell and Sons, 1970–83).
4. *The Diary of John Evelyn*, ed. E. S. de Beer, 6 vols (Oxford: Clarendon Press, 1955).
5. Edward Hyde, Earl of Clarendon, *The History of the Rebellion and Civil Wars in England*, ed. W. Dunn Macray, 6 vols (Oxford: Clarendon Press, 1888).
6. *The Memoirs of the Honorable Sir John Reresby, Baronet* (London, 1734).
7. *Bishop Burnet's History of His Own Time*, 2 vols (London, 1724 and 1734).
8. David Hume, *The History of England*, ed. W. B. Todd, 6 vols (Indianapolis: Liberty Fund, 1983).
9. Charles James Fox, *A History of the Early Part of the Reign of James the Second; with an Introductory Chapter* (London, 1808).
10. Thomas Babington Macaulay, *The History of England from the Accession of James the Second*, 4 vols (London, 1848–55).
11. J. R. Jones, *The First Whigs: The Politics of the Exclusion Crisis 1678–1683* (London: Oxford University Press, 1961); J. R. Jones, *The Revolution of 1688 in England* (London: Weidenfeld and Nicolson, 1972).
12. W. A. Speck, *Reluctant Revolutionaries: Englishmen and the Revolution of 1688* (Oxford: Oxford University Press, 1988); Tim Harris, *Revolution: The Great Crisis of the British Monarchy, 1685–1720* (London: Allen Lane, 2006).
13. Steve Pincus, *1688: The First Modern Revolution* (New Haven and London: Yale University Press, 2009).
14. John Miller, *James II* (New Haven and London: Yale University Press, 2000).
15. Scott Sowerby, *Making Toleration: The Repealers and the Glorious Revolution* (Cambridge, Mass.: Harvard University Press, 2013).

Picture Credits

1. Sir Anthony Van Dyck, *The Five Eldest Children of Charles I* (detail), 1637 (Royal Collection Trust © Her Majesty Queen Elizabeth II, 2014/Bridgeman Images)

2. Sir Peter Lely, portrait of James II when Duke of York, *c.*1665 (Royal Collection Trust © Her Majesty Queen Elizabeth II, 2014/Bridgeman Images)

3. Adriaen van Diest, *The Battle of Lowestoft, 3 June 1665*, *c.*1690 (The Berger Collection at the Denver Art Museum, Denver, Colorado)

4. Sir Peter Lely, portrait of James II when Duke of York with Anne Hyde, Princess Mary, later Mary II, and Princess Anne, *c.*1668–85 (Royal Collection Trust © Her Majesty Queen Elizabeth II, 2014/Bridgeman Images)

5. Nicolas de Largillière, portrait of James II, *c.*1686 (© National Maritime Museum, Greenwich, London)

6. Anon., *Titus Oates in the Pillory outside Westminster Hall*, 1687 (Museum of London/Bridgeman Images)

7. Anon., *The Seven Bishops committed to the Tower in 1688*, *c.*1688 (© National Portrait Gallery, London)

8. Anon., *The Landing of William III at Torbay, 5 November 1688*, *c.*1690 (© National Maritime Museum, Greenwich, London)

9. Medal commemorating the abdication of King James II, made in 1788 (© National Maritime Museum, Greenwich, London)

10. Jan Wyck, *The Battle of the Boyne*, 1690 (National Army Museum, London/Bridgeman Images)

PICTURE CREDITS

11. Benedetto Gennari the Younger, portrait of Mary of Modena with Prince James Stuart, 1692–3 (private collection/Philip Mould Ltd London/Bridgeman Images)

12. Repository for the brain of James II in the chapel of the former Scots College, Paris (Jebulon)

Index